Regulating
Early Years Services

Peter Baldock

ulton Publishers

London

David Fulton Publishers
2 Park Square, Milton Park, Abingdon, Oxon OX14 4RN

270 Madison Avenue, New York, NY 10016

First published in Great Britain in 2001 by David Fulton Publishers
Transferred to digital printing

David Fulton Publishers is an imprint of the Taylor & Francis Group, an informa business

British Library Cataloguing in Publication Data
A catalogue record for this book is available from the British Library.

ISBN 1-85346-743-X

Typeset by Book Production Services, London

Contents

Introduction

The general election of 1997 brought to power a government committed to the development of a national strategy for care and education services for young children. This commitment represented a crucial shift in social policy, one as significant in some respects as the creation of the National Health Service or the new social security system in the post-war years.

The plan announced in August 1999 to create a new regulatory body within OFSTED – the Early Years Directorate – provides one of the key elements in the Government's strategy. The eve of the establishment of the Directorate is a good time to examine the role that regulation has played so far in the development of early years services and could or should play in the future. This book attempts to do just that. It does not set out to offer guidance to childcare inspectors on the ways they should operate. Although I hope that what I have to say will have direct relevance to the day-to-day work of regulators, my primary objective has been to construct a critical account of the place of regulation in the development of services.

Four broad propositions underpin what is said in the book:

- the move to greater coordination and coherence of early years services is to be welcomed and should be taken still further;
- regulation must be about quality in its broadest sense and should not be restricted to the protection of children from harm;
- assessment of quality must be undertaken in a way that moves beyond the checking of specific criteria towards a comprehensive understanding of the situation of a provider;
- objectivity in assessment and regulation must not be confused with detachment.

None of these propositions is original. All of them are contentious. While I have argued for my own perspective, I have tried to describe those of others as best I can. This book is intended to aid debate rather than to summarise received wisdom.

The point at which the Early Years Directorate is about to be established may be a good one to produce a book on the regulation of young children's services. However, the timing also makes it important for the reader to bear in mind that it has been written in a changing situation. The final draft was produced at the end of January 2001. The basic outline of the new regulatory regime had become clear by then, but it is inevitable that minor changes and more detailed information on particular points will continue to become available in the period from when the book was written up to 1 September, when the Directorate is officially launched, and into the early stages of its life.

It may also be helpful to clarify some points about terminology. I use the term 'early years services' in this book to describe all those services that were regulated under the Nursery and Child-Minders Regulation Act 1948, as amended by section 60 of the Health Services and Public Health Act 1968, that are at the time of writing regulated under Part X and Schedule 9 of the Children Act 1989 and will be regulated under Part VI and Schedule 3 of the Care Standards Act 2000. People engaged in the implementation of Part X of the Children Act have been given a variety of job titles, including Registration & Inspection Officer and Under Eights Worker. OFSTED proposes to call the field staff in the Early Years Directorate 'Childcare Inspectors'. I have used that term throughout this book to describe those engaged in regulation under earlier regimes unless some other term was more appropriate in a specific context.

I owe a great deal for the ideas in this book and in many other ways to those who have been members of Sheffield City Council's Under Eights Team in the period since I joined it in 1993. In particular, I would like to thank Judy Cornwell, whose lovingly constructed archive on early years work in Sheffield was an invaluable resource, and Judy Thompson who offered comments on an earlier draft. I would also like to thank Cath Baldock, Emily Baldock, Margaret Fairclough, Janet Hassall, John Owens and Caroline Poland for their comments on earlier drafts. Their ideas and criticisms did much to help me improve on those versions.

Chapter 1
The historical background

The emergence of early years services

The regulation of early years services began, in effect, a little more than half a century ago in 1948. Those services themselves are barely more than a century old. The origins of day care for young children are obscure, but lie for the most part in the 19th century and reflected and reinforced ways in which family life was changing at that time.

At an earlier stage of our society it makes little sense to speak of early years day care. In the Middle Ages children of all social groups spent most of their first few years with their parents at work and at play. To a large extent care and supervision was shared. Children were very much involved with the adult world. They probably developed their own social life, but we get very few glimpses of it. One of the most impressive is offered by Bruegel's 1560 painting of children's games in the Kunsthistorisches Museum in Vienna, a picture whose fascination as a social document lies in the extent to which the games in which the children are engaged are familiar to us today. However, if children developed their own ways of playing and getting to grips with the world, few adults displayed an interest in it, except, perhaps, to regret the frivolity it appeared to entail. One example of the evident incomprehension shown by adults about the world of children is the rather ponderous way the children's street chant quoted by Jesus (in Matt. 11: 17) is translated in the King James Bible.

There is a sense in which childhood was invented in the 18th century. It was at that time that the wealthier classes began to create a protected, separate world for their own children. This pattern developed in the 19th century with the creation of the nursery in the affluent home, the invention of the pram, the design of clothing for children that differed radically from that of the adult world, the first commercially produced toys, the writing of many of the classics of children's literature and an increasing focus in the adult novel on the experience of childhood. Childhood was, of course, recognised as a specific stage (or two or three stages) of life in earlier times and there is enough evidence to dismiss any notion that affection for children and pleasure in their company were unknown before the modern era. What was missing was the idea of a specific world of childhood. That depended on the development of the nuclear family home as the standard unit in an urban setting. Certainly the Victorian nursery (or its cheap imitation – the children's bedroom in the better appointed working-class home) was only conceivable in the type of housing that became increasingly common in the modern era.

The nuclear family separated out not just the worlds of children and adults, but also the worlds of family life and work. The two developments were closely interconnected. They both unfolded over a long period of time. In the early stages of the Industrial Revolution home working remained a common feature and for better and for worse the children of the mass of the population were involved in assisting their parents in material production. This continued even with the development of large factories. These units of production were often close to the homes of the workforce and made use of the labour of men, women and children. As the ideal of the nuclear family began to take hold of all classes of society, so the campaign to protect children from employment grew and achieved increasing success in legislation and in public attitudes.

It was difficult, however, for working-class families to achieve the ideal of the mother who stayed at home, dependent on her husband's income, able to devote her time to home and family and it is a matter of guesswork how many mothers truly wanted things that way. Many working mothers must have found informal sources of care, but this would not have been possible for all. For the first time in history a widespread demand for children's day care was created.

'Minding schools' or 'baby farms' began to emerge in the cities without official encouragement. They provided a combination of day care and private fostering. We have little idea how widespread the practice was, the variety of ways in which women came to take on that role or the quality of the care offered. Baby farming came to attention mainly when something went wrong in a dramatic way – as happened when a baby-farmer was executed in 1870 for the murder of a child in her care. An official report of 1908 (cited in Jackson and Jackson 1979: 173) says of baby farms that 'They are often dirty and unsatisfactory, often conducted by women of the grossest ignorance.' This may well have been fair comment. What else might have been expected of an activity widely believed to be disreputable and totally without any form of state or voluntary organisation support? However, the comment was typical of many in both official and unofficial circles in the period before the First World War and it was part of a growing concern about the perceived evils of care of pre-school children outside the family.

It was in this context that the possibility of regulating baby farming was first introduced. 'There is no inspection or control,' commented the officials in the 1908 report. That there might be support and development did not occur to them. Forty years before the first legislation was introduced to regulate early years services the negative tone was well to the fore. The suppression of bad practice was not to be balanced by the encouragement of good. It is important to recognise that there was nothing inevitable about this. In several countries in southern Europe where it has become increasingly difficult in recent years for young parents to rely on the older generation for domestic childcare the result has not been a demand for the regulation of a growing childminding industry, but for the creation of proper, professional services. This was, for example, one of the primary outcomes of recent research by the CIREM Foundation in Barcelona Province (Casas i Aznar *et al.* 1998: 143).

It was at about the same time as the 1908 report that Margaret and Rachel McMillan were developing the early forms of holiday play care and nursery schools in London. They advanced the notion that new organisational arrangements were required to give children, the children of the urban poor in particular, opportunities that might have been more informally available in an earlier age. They thought in terms of the total needs of the child and it was easier for them to think in what we would now describe as integrated terms, because the differentiation of services and approaches had not yet been institutionalised.

The work and enthusiasm of such pioneers did not prevent fragmentation. The nursery school was caught between the respectable world of education and the disreputable world of baby farming. Gradually, there was an evolution towards the nursery school or class that was an integrated part of the universal school system and the day nursery run by the Public Health Board that catered for families that were failing. In the shadow of the day nurseries there lingered a few respectable voluntary agencies engaged in organised play activities and a quite unknown number of unrespectable baby farmers or (as they were now more usually known) childminders.

The economic crisis of the 1930s and the Second World War produced new difficulties for the established ideal of the nuclear family. The recruitment of mothers into industrial production to compensate for the loss of men to the armed forces created a new demand for childcare which could not be condemned. It was, however, still viewed with concern. Childminding was one of those activities that the realistic knew had to exist but which the respectable would not wish to acknowledge publicly.

Regulation by local health authorities

The decade after the end of the Second World War saw an enormous and fundamentally popular attempt to regain what was regarded as normality in everyday life.

Wartime restrictions were lifted only cautiously. Rationing was not abandoned until the early 1950s and conscription disappeared even later. There was less caution and more energy in the efforts to ensure that 'normality' did not mean a return to the slump of the 1930s, but rather a move forward to a system in which family life could flourish. The National Health Service and the social security system are now the best known of the changes that occurred. The massive house-building programme, in which local authorities were to play the leading role, was just as important in creating the pre-conditions for 'normal' family life for many people. There was particular ideological significance in the conception of the New Towns which were built under special legislation. Their construction represented a conscious effort to replicate what was seen as the ideal model of the small town. The design of the physical environment and a number of other measures were intended to foster orientation to the locality and inter-class solidarity which the rapidly developed industrial cities of the previous century and the 'ribbon' development along major roads of the inter-war years were seen as having undermined.

It was a crucial part of the ideal that was sought that fathers were expected to provide and mothers were expected to remain at home with their young children. The liberating impact caused by the turmoil of war continued to have many effects. The ideal marriage was increasingly seen in 'companionate' rather than hierarchical terms. More women expected to work after marriage and before the birth of the first child (to help pay for a home fit for children) and to return to work once the youngest child was about to leave school. The war had also left a number of widowed mothers for whom there could only be sympathy as they sought employment. However, the key assumption remained that the mothers of young children would remain at home to provide them with care. A whole body of literature was created explaining the harmful consequences that would follow if this did not happen.

In these circumstances, even though there were many areas of production that were desperately understaffed, the arrangements for nursery care that had been built up during the war were rapidly reduced and there was suspicion and hostility towards the working mother who lacked an excuse such as widowhood. There was particular concern about the very young child. Ministry of Health Circular 221/45 argued that 'the right policy would be positively to discourage mothers of children under two from going to work'. The National Health Service Act 1946 empowered local health authorities to set up day care, but this was seen as a means of helping failing families and not as a support to the working mother.

In 1947 considerable press publicity was given to several appalling accidents involving young children that arose from fires in the homes of childminders. There is no evidence that children were at greater risk in the homes of childminders than they were in their own homes or those of grandmothers and other close relatives; open fires and free-standing oil or paraffin heaters remained common until the late 1960s when they began to be replaced by central heating. It was a symptom of the pressure in favour of 'normal' family life, however, that the deaths and serious injuries reported in the press were seen as proof that childminding should be controlled rather than as evidence of the need to make improvements in the safety of ordinary homes.

Media pressure led in 1948 to the passing of the Nurseries and Child-Minders Regulation Act, creating a system of early years regulation for the first time. The Act obliged local health authorities to keep registers of nurseries and childminders, made it an offence for people to operate such services without registration and gave health authorities the power to refuse or cancel registration where persons or premises were not considered to be 'fit'.

It was significant that responsibility for regulation was given to local health authorities rather than the children's departments that were set up by an Act passed in the same year. Concern about childminders had focused on cases of accidental death, but concern for better management of fostering had been triggered by the death of Dennis O'Neill at the hands of a foster parent in 1945. The need to address the problems indicated by that case provided much of the justification for creating the new children's departments. Placing responsibility in two separate departments institutionalised the differences in focus, with staff in health departments concentrating on the prevention of accidents and infections and staff in the children's departments concentrating more on the people who would provide foster care. Thus the fragmentation that already existed between the care and education systems was replicated within the care system. Decades later an approved foster carer with whom the local authority was prepared to have a child with serious difficulties living full time could fail to meet the safety criteria required of a childminder caring for less vulnerable children for a few hours a day.

Fragmentation was one aspect of the 1948 Act. Another was its restricted scope.

'Nurseries' were defined in such a way as to exclude services provided by the state or others for reasons of medical or social care or of education. That is to say, it was the diminishing number of independent day nurseries that were to be regulated. (Pre-school playgroups were not taken into account since it was more than a decade before the first of these began to appear, mainly in the south-east of England. However, the law had been framed in such a way as to bring them within its ambit when they were first created in the early 1960s.)

'Childminders' were defined as people who received into their homes children to whom they were not related, who had not attained the age of compulsory education and who came from more than one household and also that they accepted 'reward' for this day-care service. This definition excluded a large number of childminding arrangements.

The aim of the Act was clearly to control, if not discourage, the large and ill-run 'baby farms' of popular imagination rather than to provide a regulatory framework for the day care of young children in any setting. No duty of inspection was laid upon local health authorities, but they were given significant powers to inspect where they had reason to think that unregistered care or care that had become inadequate since registration was being provided. A number of new criminal offences were created to aid them in the task of control.

The pressure that led to the creation of the 1948 Act did not continue for very long. The demand that young mothers stay at home was a popular one. The situations that led to the baby farms of Victorian England no longer existed in the same way. Hence there was little pressure on health departments to pursue the demands of the legislation rigorously. Those who applied to register were assessed and decisions were made, but there were few attempts to identify situations where illegal minding was in operation. It required another moral panic to set that in motion.

The early 1960s saw the gradual, but escalating, breakdown of many of the assumptions that had underpinned the post-war search for 'normality'. Anxiety grew over the development of a 'permissive society' characterised by a whole range of deviations, influencing and being influenced by cultural outputs in the theatre, novels, films and popular music and securing concessions in legislation on divorce and abortion in 1967.

In this context concern was expressed once again about the forms of day care being used by working mothers and attention focused on the potential for accidental harm. A report on the care of pre-school children seemed to underline the need for greater control (Yudkin 1967). A number of other changes were being considered in public health services as a holding response to demands for organisational reform in the National Health Service. As the Health Services and Public Health Bill made its way through Parliament in 1968, a section was added amending the Nurseries and Child-Minders Regulation Act. Section 60 tightened up on the process of checking on people working in day care or forming parts of childminders' households, required registration even when only one child received at least two hours' care and allowed for even stricter penalties for failure to comply with the Act. A Government Circular that followed strongly recommended the involvement of local fire services in checking on premises and that all registered services be inspected every six months. However, there was no requirement that regular inspection be instituted and many health departments (and later social services departments) chose to ignore this advice.

Section 60 extended the scope of the 1948 Act, but there was not the pressure to employ the powers it made available. After 1948 there was a lack of pressure because there was widespread support for the idea that the mother of young children should stay at home with them. After 1968 there was a lack of pressure for the reverse reason. Demand was steadily growing for day care and grew apace in the 1970s and beyond. Enforcement of the Act, especially the pro-active seeking out of illegal minders, would probably have caused more trouble than it was worth. Magistrates were reluctant to take action against day carers who had not been grossly cruel or negligent, a reluctance documented in the research by Elfer and Beasley (1991). When the new social services departments took over responsibility for the 1948 Act they inherited a legislative responsibility that seemed quite marginal.

The social services departments and the 1948 Act

The moment of transfer of responsibility for the 1948 Act to the social services departments was not an auspicious one. Within a few years of starting, the departments were in a double crisis that brought to an end the mood of celebration (among social workers at least) in which they were established. Resources became an issue. The escalating economic difficulties brought a ministerial announcement in 1976 that 'the party was over' and that automatic expansion of the departments as areas of need were identified could no longer be assumed. The other aspect of the crisis was even more fundamental. The notion of the 'problem family' that had underpinned so much of social work and the case for unified departments was disintegrating. The concept had encapsulated the idea that the inability of certain families to cope with life was a residual problem that required a mopping-up operation, now that structural social problems had found their solution in the major reforms of the Attlee Government and that the existence of such families could be explained largely in terms of individual pathology amenable to case work (Welshman 1999). Such a notion could not survive the 're-discovery of poverty' in the mid-1960s nor the self-confessed failure of researchers to match empirical evidence to operational definitions of the 'problem family' (Tonge *et al.* 1977). At the same time, the enquiry into the death of the child Maria Colwell began the shift of attention from the problem family and family support to the abusive family and, therefore, a more reactive service (Secretary of State for Social Services 1974). Tensions in the departments came to a head in the social workers strikes of 1978–9 and were reflected in the frantic post-strike search for a methodology or organisational model that would offer a firmer foundation for the departments. Behaviourist rather than psychoanalytic methods of individual case work, the 'systems approach', borrowed from American theorists, and more home-grown ideas of 'patch' and 'community social work' all failed to find a foothold and the departments came to rely increasingly on procedural consistency as a way of avoiding serious mistakes and the criticism that followed.

A second problem was that the senior management of the departments was often dominated by staff from the old children's departments which had had a particular prestige in social work circles. They themselves were heavily influenced by ideas first floated in the early 1950s about 'maternal deprivation' and its role in the generation of social pathology. They were often hostile to the idea that very young children should be in any kind of day care unless this were essential to support a family in crisis. Such views were reinforced by some research projects, such as Bryant *et al.* (1980) and barely offset by the efforts of those such as Raven (1981) who felt that sweeping generalisations were being made on the basis of too little evidence. This made them reluctant to invest in work on regulation beyond the absolute minimum of activity the law demanded and many departments were reluctant to meet even that statutory obligation to the full.

Then there were the unintended consequences of the commitment to 'generic' working shown by many of the departments in their first decade. Few of them organised their structures in relation to client groups. At the same time few organised themselves in relation to geographical areas alone. There were too many small and specialised services for that to be possible. Instead it became common for the principal organisational division in the departments to be one between field social work on the one hand and residential and day care on the other. This meant that any connection between the day nurseries the departments had also taken over from the old health authorities and those fieldworkers engaged in childcare inspection was impeded by the organisational structure. Often such cooperation did not happen at all and both sides missed the opportunity to learn from each other as a result. It was also rare for those with a nursery nursing background to rise very far in the hierarchies of the departments and this further diminished any influence they had on policy making.

One final factor influencing implementation of the 1948 Act was that the departments had to face major organisational change soon after their establishment because of the reforms of both local government and the National Health Service that took place in 1974.

In these circumstances it was not surprising that relatively little attention was paid to a statutory responsibility that had been seen as marginal even before the transfer. Brian Jackson's team, which was researching the topic of childminding in a number of northern local authorities in the latter part of the 1970s, found a widespread minimal approach and a failure on the part of officers to understand wider concepts of the welfare of the child. Some of the comments they quote illustrate this graphically: 'We just administer the Act'; 'What do I know about childminders? I know the Act and I carry it out'; 'The educational side doesn't come into it at all – that's not in the Act' (Jackson and Jackson 1979: 40). This seems to have been the general pattern. There were, of course, exceptions, but where departments did take more positive steps the initiative often came from junior staff rather than forming part of the strategic thinking of management. Those steps usually concerned the move away from the focus on physical health that had characterised work in the public health departments towards a broader understanding of children's welfare, including an appreciation of the potential contribution sponsored day care could make to family support strategies and a growing awareness of child protection issues. There was less understanding of curriculum issues, though staff in some social services departments were able to achieve good working relationships with under-fives advisory services in the local education departments, especially in response to the joint DES/DHSS reports *Low Cost Day Provision for the Under Fives* (1976) and *Combined Nursery Schools and Day Centres* (1977) and Joint Circulars on coordination of local authority services (1976) and coordination of all services for children (1978).

Part X of the Children Act 1989

In 1989 Parliament passed the Children Act, a comprehensive piece of legislation, Part X of which revised the law on the regulation of early years services. Of course, Part X did not represent a completely new start. A comparison of the texts shows how much of the 1948 Act was simply incorporated into the new one. There were two principal changes. The advice that local authorities inspect at six-monthly intervals was replaced by a specific requirement in section 76(4) that registered services should be subject to inspection at least once a year. The age range of children whose services were to be regulated was extended from 0–5 years to 0–8 years by section 71. A further change was that the position on exemptions from registration was considerably clearer in Schedule 9 of the Children Act than it had been in section 8 of the 1948 Act.

These were significant changes, but it is not immediately obvious why Part X should have been seen by most local authorities as a revolution in the system of regulation rather than an extension of what was already in place. There were two closely linked reasons for this. One was that children's day care was now much more on the public agenda. The other was that Part X was part of a comprehensive piece of legislation of vital importance to the social services departments.

The demand for childcare escalated in the 1980s as a result of changing patterns in family life and employment, in particular a major shift in attitudes to paid work by mothers of young children. Apart from some expansion in nursery classes in maintained schools, there was little that most local authorities could do to meet demand. New opportunities were created for the private and voluntary sectors. The number of independent nurseries (as well as nurseries and crèches attached to academic and training institutions) began to grow exponentially. After-school clubs, which had barely existed before, were created in an increasing number of places, often with central government funding made available through Training and Enterprise Councils. The number of informal, small-scale community-based holiday playschemes declined, but more elaborate holiday playcare provision was being created. The Conservative Government, which believed firmly that childcare was a private matter for families, welcomed the fact that provision was being made outside the state, but felt that parents needed the assurance of a more effective regulatory regime. The public's demand for more childcare was complemented by pressure from early years interest groups to ensure the quality of the provision being created. Unlike the legislative changes of 1948 and 1968, Part X was not produced in a context of moral panic hostile to the provision of day care for children.

There was another contrast. The 1948 Act was a brief piece of legislation on a specific issue. Section 60 was a single section all but lost in a comprehensive piece of legislation. Part X was a major part of an Act which itself re-focused the statutory framework for intervention in family life. This had two effects. One was that senior managers in the social services departments, who were having to get to grips with all that the Children Act implied for the way they operated, were more likely to take notice of it. Department of Health advice on Part X was to be found within the Guidance and Regulation on the Act as a whole. That guidance was supplemented by the detailed training pack for registration and inspection officers commissioned by the Government from the National Children's Bureau (Early Childhood Unit 1991). Social services departments were helped to work out how regulation could be conducted to a much greater extent than the health authorities had been in 1948 and 1968.

It was not just the fact that Part X had a prominent place in a major piece of legislation that gave it a more positive profile. Some of the more progressive aspects of the Act led commentators to regard the whole thing in a favourable light. Jackson believed that 'The implementation of the Children Act 1989 marked a decisive shift in philosophy from child rescue to family preservation and this had more impact on children under 5 than any other age group' (Jackson 1994: 119). Similarly, Pugh claimed that volume 2 of the 1991 Guidance and Regulations 'goes further than previous government guidance in looking at curriculum issues and equal opportunities as well as the number of toilets and amount of floor space' (Pugh 1996: 23).

All this led those charged with implementing Part X and Schedule 9 to see it as a significant opportunity.

In a majority of local authorities staff charged with responsibility for implementing Part X were located in the new 'arms length inspection units' being created in the social services departments to inspect a range of residential and day-care services. Indeed, there was a widespread belief that the Department of Health wanted authorities to locate staff in the units, though there is no documentary evidence that this was ever the case (Save the Children 1995: 11–12). In fact, senior civil servants at an NSPCC national conference and at a meeting of the Under Fives Information Service in Sheffield in 1991 specifically questioned whether the units provided the best organisational location. A significant minority of social services departments placed the staff within their main fieldwork services. In both cases staff attempting to get to grips with a new range of responsibilities were often disrupted by organisational change within the departments in which they worked. In a few cases local authorities, responsive to the growing demand for closer collaboration between departments in this field, decided to transfer their childcare inspectors and certain other staff to 'integrated' young children's services within their education departments, something Strathclyde had done as long ago as 1986 (Penn 1994).

Wherever their organisational location, there was a wide variation in responsibilities among staff. Some were specialised by the category of provider with which they dealt. Others were not. In rural authorities it was common for the same officer to deal with the inspection of residential and day-care services for adults, children's homes and children's day care within a given area. Sometimes registration, on the one hand, and inspection, investigation and enforcement, on the other, were handled by different officers. Childcare inspection teams also differed from authority to authority in the structural relationships they were supposed to have with other areas of activity, such as development and general support, the planning and delivery of training for childcare workers, direct provision of day nurseries by the SSD, child protection, fostering or preventive social work and family support. With these variations in staffing structures and responsibilities it was not surprising that salaries varied. The highest salary of which I am aware was twice as high as the lowest. It was not always clear that this variation matched differences in level of responsibility. Some salary arrangements were irrational. Those who chose to pay the staff regulating childminders less than those dealing with group care services displayed little appreciation of the significance of childminding within the network of services or the particular complexities of inspecting or supporting home-based childcare workers.

Although Part X was seen by most as a great improvement on the previous legislation and the quality of guidance issued or sponsored by central government was far better, there were problems with the new law.

The one on which most attention was fixed was the continued use of the term 'fit person'. Many regretted that the Act had not been more precise. However, in most local authorities staff had comparatively little difficulty in arriving at what appeared to be satisfactory operational definitions. The concerns about the meaning of 'fitness' reflected in part the anxiety of some staff about their ability to make judgements on people and situations rather than to measure adherence to standards, uncertainty about the extent of enforcement powers and, in particular, haziness about the circumstances in which a person could be considered for 'disqualification' under Schedule 9 of the Act. There were some complications in the matter of judging fitness. One was that the wide range of courses and formal qualifications made it problematic even for those expert in the field to determine whether proposed staff had a level of professional development that made them fit for the positions they sought. For much of the 1990s, local authorities differed widely in their approach to the question of formal qualifications, especially in relation to more community-based provision, such as preschools and after-school clubs.

Another difficulty arose in relation to checking the potential risks some persons might present. In this respect Home Office Circular 47/93 (on the conduct of checks by local authorities with local Criminal Records Offices) gave guidance that was unhelpful, even bizarre, and reflected the worries of chief constables that their administrative staff might be overwhelmed rather than reflecting a concern for the welfare of children. Local authorities had to try to negotiate deals, in effect, with local Criminal Records Offices, something rendered complicated in many circumstances by the fact that the uniformed officers in charge of those units were often at the beginning of their careers or winding down to retirement and did not remain in those particular posts for long.

Then there was the widespread uncertainty as to which services for younger primary school age children were covered by the law. The Act was clearer on activities based within schools than the 1948 Act had been. Even so, many head teachers or boards of governors claimed exemption for after-school clubs (and hard-pressed childcare inspectors were often happy to accept this reduction in their workload) before the DfEE clarified that this should not be happening, in the summer of 1998. Practice varied widely from local authority to local authority as to whether group activities offering young children training in particular aspects of the arts or sport were covered.

Another problem concerned the definition of full day care as care offered for more than four hours on any one day. This was clearly intended to describe full day-care nurseries, but summer playschemes also fell within the definition. While many of them were elaborate, well-funded holiday playcare schemes that could afford to pay the higher registration and inspection fees, others were modest community-based schemes operating for two or three weeks a year on very low budgets, often taking place in areas of multiple disadvantage. The process and cost of registration were a threat to them. There were also issues as to whether shoppers' and other crèches taking children for limited periods in the case of any individual child or community playgroups with morning and afternoon sessions were to be subject to full day-care definitions.

There were also problems arising from the different standards on staff:child ratios and space requirements in the guidance issued under Part X of the Children Act and under education legislation. It was possible for a school to use a room for children all day long only to be told by the childcare inspector that it did not meet the standards required for an after-school club for a smaller number of much the same children for two to three hours at the end of the day. The Conservative Government considered reconciling these discrepancies, but ducked the issue. Though its approach has been cautious, the Blair Government has at least begun to tackle it.

One problem which everyone more or less ignored was that Part X was so framed that the only way a provider could leave the register was to accept cancellation of the registration, but this meant that, strictly speaking, the provider could never be registered again. Most local authorities were unaware of this or found ways round it and cheerfully allowed childminders back onto the register after they had chosen to cancel and then wished to return to minding a couple of years later. Similarly, there was no provision for suspension from the register in situations where an authority could neither maintain its confidence in a provider because concerns had arisen or allegations had been made nor justify de-registration because investigation had not yet proved the provider unfit. In this particular case a judgment in the High Court (*H v Surrey County Council and CW and MW* 20 January 1994) clarified that local authorities did have a power to suspend that was implicit, though not explicit, in the legislation.

The *Surrey* case also raised, without really resolving, one final problem: that of the release of information about registered providers to parents. It was clear that the register was a public document, but childcare inspection teams held much more information on what was happening in registered services and the question was whether they had the right or the responsibility to reveal this to parents using those services or thinking of doing so. The *Surrey* judgment implied that it was acceptable for local authorities to withhold information from parents, but that questions must be answered frankly and honestly. Many felt this to be an impossible position and the attempt by Lane (1996) to address the problem only served to show how complicated and unclear the situation was. The issue of information to parents was critical for many local authorities in relation to annual inspection reports which a 1994 Government Circular suggested should be available to the public, raising issues of confidentiality and questions about the purpose of the reports.

With all these weaknesses in the legislative framework and the pressures caused by the significant expansion in group care services of all kinds, it was not surprising that a number of conflicts arose. Things proved particularly difficult in the first couple of years after implementation in 1991.

There were some complaints that regulation was proving too restrictive. Most of these were probably generated by the anxiety that the first inspections caused on both sides. The inspectors were either totally new to the field or had worked in posts with an advisory or supportive focus before and approached the first inspections with some trepidation themselves. Providers who had not been subject to this more formal type of inspection before (and in the case of private nurseries had invested considerable financial and emotional capital in projects) felt under threat. The situation in which two people or sets of people beset by anxiety had to deal with each other was loaded with potential for misunderstanding and conflict. It was a testimony to the essential reasonableness of most of them that more disputes did not arise. Some inspectors, including people who had line managed group care units themselves, had difficulty in grasping the scope and limits of their authority as inspectors. There were examples of attempts to impose very detailed requirements in ways that were officious and unhelpful.

Concern led the government to issue a Circular (LAC 1993/1) in January 1993 expressing the view that some local authorities had not been sufficiently encouraging or flexible in their approach and condemning the action of those authorities that imposed standards (particularly in relation to staffing levels) that were more stringent than those in volume 2 of the Guidance and Regulations (1991). It spoke of the Government's wish to encourage the expansion of day-care facilities, said that local authorities 'should be informed by their perception of local need as well as by the department's guidance' and reinforced the message that there was a presumption under the Act that registration would be granted unless there was good reason not to do so.

Perhaps the Circular itself was a little strident in tone. The points it made were for the most part reasonable and did not deserve the response from some quarters that childcare inspectors were being undermined and rendered incapable of doing their job. That fear was reinforced, however, by decisions in the High Court. In 1994 a nursery proprietor won a reversal of a decision by the local magistrates' court to grant the local authority immediate disqualification of the provider under section 75 rather than go through the normal process of de-registration under section 74. It seems evident that the local authority had acted precipitately in attempting to use the emergency powers of section 75 instead of the normal de-registration procedures. The outcome of this ill-advised step was that the nursery was allowed to re-open. The judgment, which concerned whether the most appropriate procedure was employed, was widely interpreted in social work circles as a failure to support the childcare inspectors in their duty to protect children. Jackman (1994) quotes a number of people to that effect. In 1995 another High Court hearing reinforced the fact that volume 2 of the Guidance and Regulations (1991) did not form part of the legislation (in relation to smacking by childminders in particular). Again, there was an outcry. Yet in retrospect it appears clear that the local authority in the case had shot itself in the foot by focusing on the status of the Guidance instead of the overall quality of service provided by the minder concerned. Some local authorities in panic withdrew their embargo on the use of physical punishments by childminders even though the High Court decision had made clear that local authorities could still impose such a requirement under section 73 if they were prepared to defend it in particular cases in the courts.

Problems with the legal framework were aggravated in many places by staff shortages resulting from budget difficulties The feeling that inspection staff were in an impossible position was reinforced by negative publicity that resulted from the deaths of young children while in the care of childminders in Sheffield, Kirklees and Norfolk and the death by accidental drowning of another young child at a private nursery in Lancashire. There was also the impact of the decision by the Parliamentary

Commissioner (the Ombudsman) in 1994 to award compensation to a woman who had experienced considerable delays in her assessment for registration as a child-minder in London.

Controversies over the application of Part X mirrored other controversies over child protection in the late 1980s and early 1990s. Social workers felt trapped in a position where intervention in families over which there was concern was seen as brutal and intrusive (Cleveland, Orkney). However, failure to have intervened strongly in situations where children had been killed was seen as evidence of weakness and incompetence (Kimberley Carlile, Jasmine Beckford, Tyra Henry). Those childcare inspectors that were in social services departments were more likely to feel the law had placed them in a no-win situation than the minority who had been transferred to education departments. The latter saw themselves even before the 1997 election as being part of an expanding and exciting field of development.

The political context of the first few years after implementation of Part X was critical. Although the concerns expressed about the actions of some local authorities in the January 1993 Circular were reasonable, they did come from a government committed to de-regulation across the board. In fact, a letter from the Department of Health in August 1993 floated the idea that there might no longer be a need for the Registered Homes Act 1984 which regulated residential care for the elderly and other adults. Reaction to the document led to that particular idea being dropped, but the very fact that it should have been raised demonstrated the readiness of the Government to consider de-regulating services for the most vulnerable. There was a widespread fear that they might be prepared to accept care for young children that was not of high quality if this made things easier for providers at a time when demand for childcare was rising but there was reluctance to invest in statutory provision.

The political context changed drastically with the general election of 1997 and the development that followed shortly afterwards of a National Child Care Strategy.

Chapter 2

The creation of the Early Years Directorate

The National Child Care Strategy

When the Labour Party won the general election in 1997 it was recognised that this would bring about some changes in relation to early years services. Few appreciated then quite how significant the scale of change would be. It is a measure of how far things have moved that we are now seeing criticism that the change has not gone far enough (Moss 2001).

The new government devised a National Child Care Strategy as the context for a number of specific reforms and initiatives (DfEE 1998). They also had a strategy for the development of pre-school education. In principle this was separate, but the inter-connections between the childcare and the education strategy were so intricate that the two strategies might as well be considered as one. Indeed, attempts by the DfEE to retain the distinction between care and education in both their funding regimes and their guidance to and requests for statistical information from local authorities caused avoidable complications in the operation of the strategy.

New Labour did not (as the Labour Party had planned to do had it won a general election in the 1980s) orchestrate a massive expansion in direct provision by local authorities. There remained, nevertheless, a considerable contrast between their approach and that of the previous Government. While the Conservatives had always had some reservations about the growth of childcare services, Labour considered that growth to be good because it freed up parents for work and training (hence reducing dependency on welfare) and provided children with an essential start in education. While the Conservatives had seen day care for children as a matter essentially for parents, Labour saw it as the duty of the state to make services available to all and not just to those whose parents could afford to meet the costs themselves or those whose drastic need was such as to justify specific intervention. This did not mean that the state had to provide all the services itself, merely that it had to create the environment in which good quality care became available universally and in ways that offered parents diversity and choice.

The overall strategy has four principal elements.

The first is the coordination of services at local level. The reliance on market mechanisms of the old nursery voucher scheme has been replaced by a greater emphasis on cooperation, involving the statutory, voluntary and commercially organised sectors. Specifically, this means that each local authority has been asked to take the lead in establishing an Early Years Development and Childcare Partnership which in turn has had to produce and implement a plan for the development of local services. Both the partnerships and their plans have to conform to government guidance (DfEE 1997). The early years plans could be seen as a natural development of the section 19 reviews of local services required by the Children Act. It is the fact that they have to be produced by properly constituted partnerships that makes them different. This is in line with other Government initiatives, including the 'Compact' with the voluntary sector. A small number of local authorities, mainly those that had established integrated early years services, found themselves in familiar territory, even if the amount of monitoring and forward planning demanded by the Government created a significant additional workload. In most local authorities the fact that the Government wished to move from rhetoric about partnership to effective mechanisms generated some degree of culture shock. This shock was, however, cushioned by the fact that local early years partnerships have usually been unconstituted bodies and have not, therefore, been able to take on full responsibility for fund management or for staffing and other resources. This has helped to keep the independent sector in the more clearly subordinate position with which most local authorities are comfortable. The other way in which the plans differ from the section 19 reviews is that the lead responsibility has been given to education departments. The health service and (within local authorities) the social and leisure services departments have a subordinate role. The Government has heeded advice offered over several years that responsibility for a more integrated approach should be given to education.

The second way the Government has sought to create the desired environment is by funding assistance offered to both parents and providers. Parents are helped to afford good quality pre-school education by the Nursery Grant Scheme administered by education departments in collaboration with local partnerships. They are also assisted with the costs of childcare through the Working Families Tax Credit (introduced in October 1999) which replaced and extended the 'childcare disregard' in the former Family Credit benefit and by the childcare grants for students in higher education announced early in 2001. Plans for accreditation schemes for out-of-school services for children over eight (which are outside the scope of childcare regulation) will increase the number of parents able to access financial assistance with childcare through the tax system. Providers have been helped to get new developments off the ground through a variety of schemes, including the New Opportunities Fund and the 'start-up' grants for new childminders which were announced early in 2000. In addition, many providers have benefited from the Single Regeneration Budget (SRB) programme or from European Union-funded programmes, including the European Social Fund (ESF) and Objective One funding. The SRB programme and ESF were available before May 1997, of course, but the Blair Government's approach to childcare has created an atmosphere in which the place of childcare in regeneration is more readily recognised and thus the opportunities are greater. The Government has also been responsible for the introduction of Education Action Zones, Health Action Zones, the Sure Start programme, the Children Fund and the Neighbourhood Nurseries Initiative, all of which have entailed assistance to childcare as a primary or subordinate part of their programmes.

The third type of measure has been investment in training, development and support. A National Early Years Training Organisation was established in 1999. A 'National Training Framework' is being created which is intended to resolve the confusion created by the large number of training initiatives in the 1980s and 1990s, thus helping childcare workers to make informed career decisions and providers to develop more coherent recruitment and professional development policies for their staff. One of the weaknesses of that framework is that early years teaching qualifications will not come within its ambit, an example of the reserve much of the teaching profession still feels towards the moves towards more integrated early years services. The Qualifications and Curriculum Authority has devised 'Early Learning Goals' for a Foundation Stage in Education, providing a revision of the Desirable Learning Outcomes devised for the original nursery voucher scheme (QCA and DfEE 2000). A number of 'centres of excellence' in early years services have been recognised and given funding. Providers eligible to receive children under the nursery grant scheme are to be assisted with the appointment of Special Educational Needs Coordinators and in securing the involvement of teachers in the development of their service. Money is coming from central government for training initiatives and the employment of development workers and advisers, often appointed by provider networks such as the Pre-School Learning Alliance (PLA) and the National Day Nurseries Association (NDNA). Finally, the Government has given enthusiastic backing to accreditation schemes which endorse the work of particular providers.

The fourth method of creating the right environment has been the improvement of the system for regulating early years services. The Protection of Children Act 1999, which came into force in October 2000, lays much clearer obligations on those engaging people to work with children in relation to the checks they must conduct. The DfEE in conjunction with the Social Services Inspectorate and others began in 1999 to construct a comprehensive set of standards for early years services. A consultation pack was issued in August 2000. The Social Services Inspectorate conducted a detailed examination in 2000 of the work of childcare inspection teams. These were not initiatives that had simply come about at random. All of them were linked to the proposal to remove responsibility for the regulation of early years services from local authorities to a new national body.

The move to a new regulatory regime

In 1998 the Department of Health and the DfEE produced a joint consultation paper on the regulation of early education and day care. The paper gave some indication of the Government's thinking and asked 39 specific questions.

The range of issues addressed was wide. They included the question of which services should come within the scope of regulation, the expectations there should be on owners and managers of facilities, special educational needs, the standards that should be set, the arrangements for recruiting, training and allocating work to inspectors, the relationship between regulation and supportive work, the question of whether there should be improved national monitoring of standards, the role of accreditation schemes, the relationship between overall regulation and child protection and the system of registration and inspection fees that had been introduced under the Children Act. Many who responded focused on issues of standards and exemptions. Others had views on the relationship between regulation and support. Not many homed in on what was probably the most important question, tucked away quietly as number 21: 'Should regulation be organised locally or nationally by a body such as OFSTED? Are there other possibilities?'

When the Early Years Division at the DfEE reported on the outcome of the consultation in January 1999 the possibility of a new organisational framework for regulation was still not highlighted. It was appreciated in some quarters that change was likely, but even those people did not see where the Government's thinking was leading. The social work profession assumed that, if responsibility for Part X of the Children Act were transferred, it would be to the new Care Commission which it was planned to establish in April 2002 and which would have a range of responsibilities, including regulation of residential homes for children and adults. This was a little naive. It displayed a failure to understand the strength behind the lobbying that had been conducted for nearly two decades to lodge responsibility for early years work in the sphere of education rather than social services.

Whether people wanted early years regulation to stay with local authorities, to transfer to the Care Commission in 2002 or to come under some other arrangement, few followed up the results of the 1998 consultation by promoting or engaging in proper debate about the best possible organisational framework for registration, inspection and enforcement. It therefore came as a surprise when on 2 August 1999 Margaret Hodge on behalf of the Government announced that responsibility would be transferred to OFSTED.

The timing of the announcement – in the middle of the holiday period – meant that there was less immediate reaction than there might have been, but such reaction as there was took an almost overwhelmingly hostile and critical form. The unexpectedness of the decision had something to do with this. There were other factors.

For some people this was another nail in the coffin of local democracy which had been systematically undermined by the Thatcher and Major Governments and which the Blair Government was attempting to reinvigorate by the creation of new institutions in Scotland, Wales and London rather than by the restoration of powers to existing authorities. Even those who were critical of the way local government operated might ascribe importance to local structures amenable to local influences. One former inspection manager stated '... there would be something truly suspect (if not downright sinister) if every inspector worked in exactly the same way. A good reason ... to be worried over the announced move of children's day care regulation to OFSTED' (Hopkins 2000: 4).

Other people had concerns about OFSTED itself. It had received negative publicity for what was seen as the aggressive and intrusive nature of its inspection system. The former schools inspection system, which it replaced, had already moved, since the creation of the Schools Council in 1962, from an approach based on work with individual teachers and schools to a more considerable role in the development of national education policy. OFSTED was seen as something different again, as being committed to both prescription and detachment in a way that made teachers 'objects of the inspection process, not participants in it' (Maw 1996: 23). Many childcare inspectors and providers did not want that kind of approach.

However, the greatest strength of feeling came from those who resented the transfer of responsibility from the social work to the education profession. Some of this came from community-based providers (including many childminders) who feared that the transfer would entail a shift in a more explicitly educational direction that they did not want to take. The most aggressive comment came from the social work profession itself. Michael Hake of the Association of Directors of Social Services published an angry diatribe in the *Guardian*. In the weeks that followed, the journal *Community Care* quoted outraged statements from a number of sources. The strength of feeling was considerable, but there was little to sustain it. In the event, the sound and fury were not followed by any serious attempt to reverse the decision.

The Care Standards Act 2000

The transfer to OFSTED required a change in the law and there were also a number of weaknesses in Part X and Schedule 9 of the Children Act that could usefully be put right. The Government chose the vehicle of the Care Standards Bill which it was preparing as the legislative base for the National Care Standards Commission.

The bill received the royal assent in July 2000. Part VI and Schedule 3 deal with the arrangements for the regulation of childminding and day care, replacing the previous provisions of the Children Act in this respect.

There are significant aspects of the previous legislation that have not changed, just as Part X of the Children Act incorporated a good deal that had been in the 1948 and 1968 legislation. The principal changes are the transfer of responsibility to the Chief Inspector in England (with comparable arrangements in Wales), new arrangements for appeals against the decisions of the regulator, clarification of several issues that had arisen in the period since implementation of the previous legislation in 1991, the creation of new responsibilities and powers for the regulator and new obligations imposed on local authorities.

The Act transfers responsibility for the regulation of childminding and children's day care from local authorities in England and Wales to Her Majesty's Chief Inspector of Schools in England and the National Assembly for Wales in that country. (In what follows I shall refer to the Chief Inspector alone. The powers of the National Assembly in Wales are parallel. The Act leaves unchanged the situation in Scotland.)

- The Chief Inspector is required to create a register of childcare inspectors (section 79P (1)). (This register may be combined with the Register of Inspectors established under the School Standards and Framework Act 1998.)
- The Chief Inspector may exercise powers of inspection either directly through staff employed within OFSTED or by making arrangements with others (section 79Q (4)).
- In certain circumstances OFSTED may invite someone who is not a registered inspector to conduct an investigation (section 79U (5)). (The most likely example of this would be investigation by the SSD of concerns about a registered provider relating to child protection.)

The Act makes new provision for appeals against decisions of the regulator.

- The Tribunal established under section 9 of the Protection of Children Act will hear appeals against Early Years Directorate decisions to refuse registration, to de-register or to suspend from registration (sections 79M and 79H (2)). (This procedure largely replaces the appeals to the courts established under the Children Act, but the Human Rights Act could open the way to appeals against Tribunal decisions.)

The Act clarifies a number of issues that had arisen since the implementation of Part X of the Children Act.

- The meaning of 'childminder' is further clarified by the statement that 'any day on which he does not act as a childminder at any time between 2 a.m. and 6 p.m. is to be disregarded' (section 79 (8)).
- The Care Standards Act specifies more clearly than the Children Act which staff in group care provision are to be taken into account in judging suitability (section 79B (5)).
- Provision for temporary suspension of a provider from the Register is now explicit (section 79H (1) and (2)).
- There is now provision for providers to cancel of their own volition, opening up the way to return to the register at a later date (section 79J (1)).
- There was no requirement in the Children Act for inspections to be followed by written reports, although that practice became universal. The Care Standards Act

specifies that reports must be produced within prescribed intervals and empowers the Chief Inspector to make them partly or wholly available to the public (section 79R).

- An applicant for registration faced with a refusal to register will not be allowed to withdraw the application so as to make fresh application possible in the future (section 79E (4)).

The Act creates new powers and responsibilities for the new regulatory regime.

- The Act speaks of applicants being 'qualified' rather than 'fit'. This may not seem any more precise a term, but the intention is to place the onus on the applicant having to prove suitability rather than the regulator having to prove it on the balance of probabilities. This lays the basis (along with transfer to a single national body in England) for a more coherent approach to refusal to register and de-registration (sections 79B and 79F).
- The exemptions from registration available to children's day care in residential units and hospitals are abolished (Schedule 3 (2)).
- The Secretary of State may determine the intervals at which inspections will be conducted, i.e. they need no longer be conducted annually (section 79Q).
- The annual inspection fees are replaced by annual re-registration fees which may be collected by administrative process unconnected with inspection (Schedule 3 (7)).
- The Chief Inspector is empowered to 'secure the provision of training for persons who assist in providing childminding or day care or intend to do so' (section 79N (4)). (One of the issues is whether Early Years Directorate will set up its own pre-registration courses or rely on the Introduction to Childminding Practice courses devised by the National Childminding Association (NCMA) and attracting CACHE accreditation.)
- The Chief Inspector is empowered to establish a system under which people running services for children over eight that would be required to register if any of them were under eight will have to seek 'certificates of suitability' (section 79W).

The Act creates new obligations on local authorities to provide information on day-care services and training for people providing care. Guidance and regulations on both these topics will be issued to local authorities early in 2001.

- Local authorities are now required (as opposed to permitted under the Children Act) to provide information to parents on childcare services in their areas (section 79V (a)).
- Similarly, local authorities are now required to promote training in childcare, something also required under the guidance for Early Years Development & Childcare Plans 2001–4 (section 79V (b)).

A great deal that is in Part VI and Schedule 3 of the Care Standards Act does not differ from the provisions of Part X and Schedule 9 of the Children Act (except in so far as the regulatory body has changed).

- There is still the need for separate registrations for separate services offered by the same provider.
- The Secretary of State still has the power to introduce new regulations (section 79C).
- There is still a range of criminal offences which may arise if there is failure to comply with the legal requirements of the regulator (sections 79C (7), 79D (4), 79D (6), 79E (5), 79F (6), 79U (7), 79W (6) and (7), Schedule 9A para. 5).
- The term 'requirement' in the previous legislation has been replaced by the term 'condition of registration' but it remains to be seen whether this will prove to be a mere change of terminology or a change with more significance (sections 79B (3) and (4), 79F (3) and (6)).
- The right of the regulator remains in place to apply to the courts for emergency closure of a provision or variation of the requirements laid on it if there is evidence it is being run in a way that has caused or might cause significant harm to one or more children (section 79K).
- The processes under which the regulator gives notice of intention to refuse, cancel or vary the conditions of registration remain the same (section 79L).

There are, however, areas which have not changed, but where there had been some demand for reform.

- The two-hour limit remains in place, i.e. if a provision operates for less than two hours on any one day it is exempt from registration.
- There has been no further attempt to clarify the differences between child-minding sponsored by social services departments and fostering arrangements, although the term 'fostering' is itself defined in a revised manner in the Act.
- There is no clarification of the situation where a succession of different providers use the same premises, but each claims to be an occasional user, e.g. where a conference centre has space used for crèche facilities regularly, but responsibility for them rests with the conference organisers rather than the conference centre.
- There has been no attempt to review the situation of services which do not come within the ambit of the 'five days rule', but are not long-term provision, e.g. the crèche attached to a six-session course run in a local church hall or other social centre.
- There has been no attempt to close those loopholes that allow some providers to evade registration by describing themselves as schools or as integral parts of independent schools when to all intents and purposes they are operating as full day-care nurseries.

In addition to defining the new regulatory regime the Act also made provision for the transfer of local authority staff already engaged in childcare inspection or its administrative support to have rights of transfer to the Early Years Directorate (sections 114 and 115).

On balance, and leaving to one side for the moment the question of which agency should have been given the regulatory powers, Part VI of the Care Standards Act is an improvement on Part X of the Children Act which had already provided an improved framework for regulation.

The national standards for the regulation of day care and childminding in England

Part X of the Children Act provided a legislative framework for regulation, but said little as to the criteria to be used by those engaged in it. Volume 2 of the Guidance and Regulations (particularly pages 32–48) gave useful advice to local authorities (and to providers as to what local authorities might reasonably expect). However, it was left very much to each local authority to devise its own detailed guidance in order to ensure internal consistency in decision making and clarify the position to applicants for registration. They differed widely in how they presented their guidelines, how specific they were and how far and in what way they made use of their powers under sections 72.5 and 73.7 to impose requirements not in the Act on all providers.

The Secretary of State had powers under section 73.4 to oblige local authorities to impose additional requirements or refrain from doing so. Thus it did not require a change in the identity of the regulatory body for the Government to produce new national standards in order to secure greater consistency in application of regulation across the country. Work began on this ahead of the passage of the Care Standards Bill. However, there was a link with the planned transfer of responsibility to OFSTED in so far as the Government wished to complete the process of consultation about new standards before the Chief Inspector assumed responsibility. The announcement that work would begin on new standards was made at the same time as the announcement that OFSTED was to take over early years regulation.

A draft pack was produced in August 2000 and consultation was conducted by a variety of means (principally by a questionnaire issued as part of the pack) in the period leading up to 31 October.

The proposal was to have five sets of standards, covering what were seen as the five broad categories of service:

- childminding;
- sessional care;
- full day care;
- crèches;
- out-of-school care.

Definitions are offered for each type of care and it is clearly hoped that these are tight enough to avoid the confusion that has arisen in some places as to the category a particular service fits and, therefore, the criteria it must meet. There is still likely to be some uncertainty. OFSTED will need to develop an internal system of 'case law precedent' to cover situations where, for example, an after-school club is established in association with a nursery school or class or where a crèche gains a regular clientele to an extent that raises doubts as to whether it is providing 'occasional care'. Distinguishing between categories has been one of the most problematic areas in the construction and revision of guidelines at local level.

Each of the 5 modules is subject to 14 standards relating to:

- the suitability of persons to provide care;
- the effectiveness of the organisation;
- the ways in which children's individual care needs are met and the planning to develop children's emotional, physical, social and intellectual capabilities;
- the suitability of the physical environment;
- the suitability of equipment;
- the promotion of safety;
- the promotion of health;
- the suitability of food and drink;
- the promotion of equality of opportunity;
- the provision to meet special needs;
- the suitability of methods of behaviour management;
- work in partnership with parents and carers;
- compliance with child protection procedures;
- effective record keeping and the development of written policies and procedures.

The criteria for each standard vary according to the module.

There were many things that were welcome about the new guidance. The material was neatly structured. It underlined the fact that the essential concerns in childcare and education remained the same throughout the whole range of settings, while allowing for the need to apply different criteria for the same standards in different settings. The 14 standards covered all the broad issues that anyone was likely to wish to see covered. The emphasis on overall judgement, risk assessment and the measurement of outcomes rather than on the application of long lists of standards that were in the strictest sense measurable was an important gain. It was also a considerable advantage that the two issues of care of babies and of overnight stays were specifically addressed. Those who had framed the guidance in volume two failed to appreciate how significant these two areas would become. That was hardly surprising. Very few people did at the beginning of the 1990s. They had, however, become increasingly important over the decade and were major sources of concern for many childcare inspectors.

The pleasant surprise that the care of babies had been highlighted as an issue was, however, overshadowed by the unsatisfactory nature of what was said. Care of children under two is one area where a raising of space and staffing standards should have been considered carefully. Concern was also felt in some quarters on other issues. For example, the rationale for differences in detail on the matter of child protection in the different modules was not obvious.

A much larger issue was that of the balance in the coverage given to different topics. Although all 14 standards have relevance to curriculum, only 1 of them – the third – highlights education either in its basic formulation or in the ways in which the specific criteria are elucidated. By way of contrast, the prevention of accidental harm is the strongest element in two of the standards – six and seven – and features heavily in four and eight. In other words, there is emphasis on prevention of harm and less on the potential benefits of early years services or on where they fall within the framework of education. (This is especially true of the module on 'out-of-school care' where the distinction between the proper activities of schools and day care provided on school premises and in association with schools is reinforced by the skimpiness of the criteria and their focus on play.)

For some people this balance was welcome. There had been many worries that the transfer of responsibility to OFSTED might lead to an undue emphasis on education. For example, after-school clubs might be forced into becoming homework support groups. OFSTED and the DfEE seem to have felt under pressure to reassure people on this score. That does not mean that the consequences of that wish to reassure make sense. The principal justification for transferring responsibility to OFSTED was that early years services and their regulation needed to be seen in an educational context. If that were not the case, why not transfer responsibility to the Care Commission (assuming that it was agreed some stronger national framework was needed for regulation and that responsibility could not be allowed to rest with local authorities)?

Another issue to which the pack gave rise was that of consistency. The 'Introduction' to the pack made a great deal of the need to dispel inconsistencies between local authorities (para. 4). However, with the emphasis that was being given to outcomes, overall standards and broadly defined criteria, it was not clear that the standards would achieve this. With the exception of the question of which qualifications were required for which settings, the most common inconsistencies between local authorities (and to some extent between Registered Nursery Grant inspectors and Children Act inspectors) were over points of very fine detail, often related to considerations of health and safety. If the standards were not to create consistency by very specific and detailed regulation on such matters as the precise height of a childminder's garden fence, then some other source of consistency had to be discovered. The solution might have come from the operational approach of the Early Years Directorate – from the precision of its procedures, the imaginative use of new technology for exchange between staff and a programme of staff development. However, the pressure for a more prescriptive approach led to the decision to work on more detailed guidance to go alongside the criteria at the beginning of 2001. That work should be completed by the spring. Whatever the preferred solution to the difficulty, it would have been welcome had it been acknowledged from the start that the pack itself raised the issue of consistency in a particularly sharp way instead of pretending that it offered a solution.

There were two issues that generated protest across the whole field of early years services.

The first was that of qualifications and experience. Volume 2 of the Children Act Guidance had suggested that 50 per cent of the staff in group care services should be qualified, but had left it to local authorities to determine the levels of qualification. The module for out-of-school care neither specified the level of qualification (in NVQ terms) nor gave any priority to playwork over other forms of qualification appropriate to caring for children. This was a cause for some concern. There was greater anxiety about the requirements for the three modules for pre-school services. In all three it was suggested that at least 50 per cent of the staff should have level II qualifications only and allowed providers to offer as an alternative some kind of guarantee that this would be achieved within a fixed period. This constituted a potential threat to some of the more informal kinds of community-based sessional care services whose staff often lacked formal qualifications. At the same time it fell far short of what most local authorities had insisted should be the requirement for full day-care services and crèches. Just as controversial was the failure to specify the length or nature of the experience that people should have before taking on managerial positions. The idea that someone could take on the running of a service having recently obtained one of the relevant paper qualifications and without extensive guided experience was seen as absurd. *Nursery World*, in its issue of 24 August 2000 launched a campaign to 'Stop the Drop in Standards', a campaign actively supported by the NDNA and a number of leading companies in the private day-nursery field. It was a measure of how badly feeling in the early years sector had been misjudged that the NDNA played so prominent a part in the campaign. This may well be the only example in history of a trade association (which the NDNA is in part) accusing the regulators of being insufficiently stringent in the standards they wished to impose.

There were equally strong feelings about the proposal that childminders should be allowed to smack minded children or smoke in their presence as long as they had the written consent of parents and later at the fact that the Government decided in December 2000 to approve this ahead of completion of the consultation process. The NCMA had run a high-profile campaign on the issue of smacking by childminders in 1994. For many there was a matter of principle about the treatment of children. There were also practical questions at stake. How would the childminder know that her definition of a smack coincided with that of the consenting parent? What would happen if some parents of a particular childminder wanted her to smack and others did not? How would the children view such a situation? Did anyone care about the fact that, as people working on their own, childminders are particularly vulnerable to accusations of abuse or to the risks of situations getting out of hand and that a strict regulation against physical punishment offers some measure of protection to them? There was also the consideration that the proposal seemed to suggest that childminders were second-rate care-givers who could not be expected to meet the same standards as other childcare workers. One of the effects of the proposal was to lead a number of experienced childminders to move out of the job. The decision was as damaging in its impact as it was puzzling in its inconsistency with policy in other areas of childcare.

Both the matter of qualifications and experience and the question of whether child-minders should be allowed to smack children or smoke in their presence with parents' consent were taken up by a Parliamentary Select Committee which came down firmly in favour of the views of the overwhelming majority of early years practitioners and against the proposed standards (Wiltsher 2001).

Finally, alarm bells were sounded by the resurrection of the phrase 'light-touch inspection' which had first been used in the context of the Nursery Voucher Scheme. That phrase is grossly dishonest because it is so vague. It suggests that little will happen in the way of detailed examination of practice or of enforcement where there are problems that merit it. It suggests these things but does not say them out loud. It leaves both the inspectors and the inspected in a situation of uncertainty in which collusion over poor standards becomes more than possible. The fears that were generated by the phrase were reinforced by the fact that the consultation pack included an assessment of some of the major financial implications of the standards for providers. That the DfEE should concern itself with this issue because of its relevance to the viability of local early years plans was reasonable. The inclusion of the document in a pack designed to consult on standards hinted at a readiness to compromise on minimum standards in order to purchase childcare on the cheap.

In other words, for all that was good in the consultation pack, there was an underlying message that the new regulatory regime would focus on prevention of manifest harm rather than the promotion of quality.

The Curriculum Guidance for the Foundation Stage

Shortly before the consultation pack was produced, the Qualifications and Curriculum Authority (QCA) brought out its Curriculum Guidance for the Foundation Stage in Education which builds on the 'Early Learning Goals' document produced by QCA in October 1999, itself a revision of the 1995 document on 'Desirable Learning Outcomes'.

The Guidance is structured around those goals describing for each of them the typical 'stepping stones' through which children can be expected to progress in the period from their third to their fifth birthdays, giving examples of things children do that illustrate these stepping stones and outlining things that practitioners can do to assist children in their learning and development. These stepping stones and the relevant types of practitioner activity are in turn divided into four phases from age three to the end of the foundation stage. The phases are indicated by colour coding rather than being described in terms of the typical age at which children might be expected to move from one phase to another. Thus there is sensitivity to the fact that development, while directional, is not precisely programmed and variation between children even from similar backgrounds and in the same settings must be expected. In this and other ways QCA have made efforts to ensure that the Guidance is seen as curriculum guidance and not as a syllabus to be followed mechanically.

Some of the ways in which the guidance differs from earlier documents also show a greater sensitivity to the needs of young children that are not 'educational' in a restricted sense of that word. The fact that there is stronger reference to emotional needs and the right of the child to respect, the addition of 'communication' to 'language and literacy', the endorsement of mere silliness in the recognition that rhyme can be for fun as well as assisting memory, the greater emphasis on special needs – these are all elements of a more 'integrated' perspective than was apparent in the proposed national standards.

It will be interesting to see how far this Guidance (and subsequent documents) impact on the process of regulation under the Care Standards Act. There is the risk that it will be seen as having relevance only to those settings that seek eligible provider status and, indeed, the fact that the definition of terms suggests that it is relevant only to those childminders who are members of approved childminding networks would seem to encourage this. (Individual childminders cannot seek eligible provider status under the Nursery Grant Scheme. This status is only available to childminders in networks accredited by the NCMA and – at the time of writing at least – they are a very small minority of the country's registered minders.) In general, the introductory part of the Guidance emphasises the relevance of what is said to eligible providers rather than others. Thus, although Margaret Hodge in her introduction to the Guidance speaks of the Government's objective of providing 'a high quality, integrated early education and childcare service for all who want it', there are implications of a separation of educational and childcare concerns.

This seems a pity. The 'packaging' of the Guidance (both its provenance and some of the language employed) means it is unlikely to be read by many childminders who choose not to join accredited networks or some of the more informal community-based playgroups. Nevertheless, few people committed to those areas of work would have difficulty in agreeing with the 'principles for early years education' summarised on pages 11–12 or would fail to benefit from some of the practical ideas in the main body of the Guidance. In the period before the Nursery Voucher Scheme was introduced, staff in some social services departments and in most of the handful of 'integrated' young children's services were working with colleagues in LEA advisory services on the relevance of the National Curriculum to an understanding of how childcare settings could help lay the foundations for later learning and development. There is room for reflection on the relevance of this Guidance to judging the capacity of providers to match the third of the new national standards

OFSTED's approach to structure and mode of operation

Devising procedures and organisational structures is an essential, if sometimes tedious, process. However, some might feel that, once standards are set, it is a relatively simple matter to send people out to judge whether or not there is adherence to them. The impact of the organisation's style of operation on those it sends out to make such judgements may receive less careful consideration.

This danger was evident in the quality of debate in the initial stage on the organisational aspects of the Early Years Directorate, the new 'arm' of OFSTED that will deal with the regulation of early years services. There was a danger at that time of avoidable conflict because many of the assumptions about organisation that were brought to the debate by the staff being transferred to the Directorate from local authorities and by staff inside OFSTED itself are so ingrained that they have hardly been articulated. This is something that could still make for continued conflict and misunderstanding.

This is a common phenomenon. Sociologists in Poland in the 1950s and 1960s developed the concept of the 'institutional model', the half-formulated set of assumptions about organisational practice that people bring from one type of setting to another. They pointed out that lessons learned in one type of organisation might have limited relevance in another, but that people with organisational experience were not necessarily aware of this. There are a number of these unconscious 'institutional models' around at present which will only be useful when fully articulated. That might be an uncomfortable experience for everyone concerned, but still a better one than mutual misunderstanding and a consequent sense of grievance.

There were misunderstandings right at the start in the autumn of 1999 following Margaret Hodge's August announcement. Many of the staff in local authorities tried in effect to get into a style of negotiation that would have been appropriate in the case of a major re-organisation within a local authority, but was quite inappropriate as a way of dealing with this situation. Staff from OFSTED and the DfEE struggled sometimes in trying to explain to anxious people that for reasons of constitutional etiquette there were considerable limits to what they could do in the way of framing organisational proposals until the Care Standards Bill was at least in its final stages.

The Bill itself gave few clues as to the organisational arrangements that would be put in place once it received the royal assent and was implemented. From the start it contained essentially two proposals on this score. It gave basic powers and responsibilities to Her Majesty's Chief Inspector (in England; and to the Assembly in Wales) and it spoke of a register of inspectors. This gave at least three options (and variations on each of those) that might be adopted by OFSTED in the creation of the new service.

The one that was always least likely was that the Chief Inspector would simply take over control of the existing operations in the 150 local authorities in England. The arrangements adopted by those authorities differed so significantly from each other that this was never a practical proposition. It would have made it impossible to secure the consistency of approach that was the primary objective of the legislation.

Nevertheless, many childcare inspectors assumed that this would be a 'transfer of undertakings' similar to the arrangements that had happened when a variety of community care services had been 'out-sourced'. At the same time providers were often being reassured by people who spoke with more confidence than the small amount of information they had could justify that nothing very much would change after the transfer and they would still be dealing with the same childcare inspectors in much the same way, though a gradual process of change could be assumed after that.

The second option was that Children Act registration and inspection teams might have become part of the advisory services within their authorities' education departments and funded their existence to a large extent by undertaking inspections on behalf of OFSTED, much as colleagues in those services funded their operations in part through undertaking school inspections outside their own areas. Many senior managers in education departments, accustomed to OFSTED's normal mode of operation, assumed this would be the case and expressed approval of the objectivity that was assumed to go with inspection of settings with which the inspector had no previous connection. On the other hand, many of those already engaged in registration and inspection work valued the continuity of contact they had (on a team basis if not an individual one) with local settings and had reservations about the school inspection model. There were also fears that, if inspection under the Care Standards Act were to be organised on a basis similar to the organisation of nursery grant inspections, then local authority units would lose out to those parts of the private sector that had a well-established base in work with registered nursery grants inspectors (RNgIs). The second model was seen as threatening on a professional and employment security basis.

The third option was to create a salaried inspectorate within OFSTED, while allowing for the possibility of commissioning work from others if the salaried inspectorate proved unable to cope with a sudden influx of work as various aspects of the National Childcare Strategy fell into place. This is the option that was eventually adopted with the proposal to create a new 'arm' of OFSTED to be called the Early Years Directorate. That the principle had been accepted was clear by the end of 1999 when the first drafts of the sections guaranteeing the right of existing staff to transfer were drafted, although it was not until July 2000 (the month in which the Bill received the royal assent) that some of the principal features of the planned Directorate became clearer.

It is easy to understand why staff in OFSTED may have had initial reservations about the idea of a salaried inspectorate. Local authorities employed something like three or four times as many people in this sphere of work as OFSTED had on its own existing workforce. No organisation can cope easily with a quadrupling of its size. In this case the group that will form the majority from September 2001 come from a significantly different professional culture, so the potential threat to the host body is all the greater. OFSTED's staff must surely have experienced some degree of resentment at the hostile reception the August 1999 announcement received in the social work press and wondered at the consequences of accepting people from a social services background into their organisation in large numbers. Some future historian will disentangle the story of such reluctance as there was within OFSTED to accept this and the thinking that led to the political decision to have a salaried inspectorate. An appreciation of the skills that could be lost if there were not one was probably a consideration. Officials from the DfEE said a great deal during the period of the passage of the Bill about how much the skills of existing childcare inspectors were valued. However, as none of them ever identified what precisely they thought these skills were, this sounded more like tact and politeness than real appreciation. The real problem was that the right to transfer was being given in the case of the National Care Commission which was always envisaged as having a salaried staff and it was impossible to grant the right of transfer in one case and not the other.

Although the principle of a salaried inspectorate was accepted, the proposals as they began to emerge were for a model that looked as little like the first option as possible. Largely on the grounds that administrative and premises costs should be kept at a minimum to ensure that there were enough fieldwork staff, OFSTED rejected the idea of establishing local offices in the area of each local authority. Childcare inspectors were to work from home. This major decision was announced without prior consultation, something that suggests a failure somewhere in OFSTED to appreciate the employee relations aspect of the question. Home-based working is notoriously difficult to introduce and something that requires careful discussion with staff. To introduce it by decree and impose it on a group of staff already being organisationally disrupted in other ways was pretty appalling practice even if in principle it made sense to have staff working from home. It was widely resented among the staff hoping to transfer as they valued the informal support and learning that resulted from office-based work, especially in large city local authorities where staff were more likely to spend time between visits to providers at their office bases than they were in far-flung rural areas. Resentment was strongest among those teams that were operating from offices which housed other agencies connected with their local partnerships. This was ironic as it was this group of childcare inspectors that might have been expected to give the move to OFSTED the greatest welcome because they had already made the transition from the social services to the education sphere. There were to be eight regional offices (each with a broadly equivalent workload) while most of the fieldwork staff would become home-based. The regions were related to the standard government regions rather than those used by the Department of Health and the Social Services Inspectorate. One consequence of this was that in certain areas (such as South Yorkshire) where the standard government regions and the Department of Health regions did not coincide the basis for closer cooperation with the Regional Care Commissions once they were established was diminished.

Some of the early comments from OFSTED staff about the new structure said little about team work or about relating the work of the Directorate to the work of local partnerships and demonstrated little appreciation of the fact that regulation in this field entailed registration, investigation and enforcement just as much as inspection. The model which some people had in mind seemed to be that of the individual inspector parachuted in from somewhere else to see what was happening and write a report. There may well have been assumptions to this effect, but as more detailed proposals emerged, it became evident that OFSTED had been listening to existing staff, providers of services and those active in the local partnerships. There was to be a team structure, each team led by a senior childcare inspector who would undertake some direct fieldwork as well as supervising others in the team. Teams themselves were to relate to partnership areas. Continuity in dealing with situations and equal weight given to registration, inspection, investigation and enforcement were accorded some value. There was a degree of responsiveness on OFSTED's part that was reassuring even if a number of difficult issues remain unresolved and it took more time than was reasonable or reassuring for OFSTED to come up with details on job descriptions, grades, conditions of service and the process of transfer.

By the summer of 2000, OFSTED had clearly accepted the principle that regulation in this field could not be a matter of inspection alone. It is not yet completely clear how they see the different aspects of regulation being interconnected. In particular, there was at the time of writing still some lack of clarity as to how they see the share of responsibility between the local childcare inspection teams and the regional offices for registration, investigation and enforcement. There had been at the start some indications that they saw registration as being largely an administrative exercise that could be conducted in the regional offices and failed to appreciate the value of the supportive way in which local childcare inspectors have approached registration applications (or the harmful consequences where they have not). More recently they have emphasised the importance of the assessment conducted by childcare inspectors in the process of registration, though this leaves unclear the extent to which this work is to be seen in comparatively supportive terms. It is also unclear how local childcare inspectors are to become involved in investigations or at what point and why they will be expected to transfer responsibility for further action to regional offices. There are very practical considerations here, but they also have a bearing on how the regulatory task is perceived. Both Elfer and Beasley (1997) and the Social Services Inspectorate (2000) had noted how much confusion there was among childcare inspection units about the circumstances in which enforcement is required. That uncertainty could increase rather than diminish if there is an uncertain division of responsibility between the local teams and their regional offices in the Early Years Directorate.

Then there is the whole issue of the integration of perspectives relating to care, education and playwork and how this will affect the work of the Early Years Directorate. The hostility of the social work establishment to the change and the frequently expressed fears that it will lead to a neglect of child protection issues may have made OFSTED back off from highlighting curriculum issues in a way that would have been useful and may also have squeezed out the perspectives of playworkers which are easily lost in the battle between the two professional giants. Of course, when the Early Years Directorate does attempt to adopt a more integrated approach to childcare inspection it will be up against a major problem of staff development. Many of the childcare inspectors being transferred will not have had to face such issues before. On the other hand, there was a similar issue when the Children Act brought out of school care for younger children into the regulatory framework and many local authorities tackled that successfully even if they struggled at first. At the risk of seeming arrogant in the eyes of some, OFSTED needed to grasp this particular nettle from the earliest stage and appeared at first to be hesitant about doing so.

Teams of childcare inspectors that are operating locally are important so that there is effective communication and cooperation with other regulatory agencies whose work impinges on this field. This includes environmental health officers, the fire and rescue service and local authority planning departments as well as social services departments and the area child protection committees. Child protection has already been made the subject of a specific protocol as a result of concerns expressed by the Association of Directors of Social Services. Similar arrangements are needed with the other agencies as well if the existing working relationships are not to break down and be replaced with confusion. Protocols themselves are only starting points and a good deal will remain to be done by the regional offices once all the formal agreements are in place.

Local childcare inspection teams are also important in terms of communication and cooperation with a range of other services within the local early years development and childcare partnerships. This includes planners, people concerned with training and quality assurance and a range of development and capacity-building staff. Such connections are needed if we agree, as I will argue in a later chapter we should, that there is a supportive element to regulation. They become even more critical if the two areas of activity are seen as quite divorced since such a demarcation will demand clear means of exchange to help each in their work. Involvement in work with local partnerships will also be important in keeping childcare inspectors abreast of developments in the field and prevent them slumping into an unthinking routine of regular inspections.

OFSTED has said clearly it intends to become an agency that makes the fullest use of new technology. The fact that childcare inspectors will be home-based rather than working from local offices makes reliance on new technology inevitable. There will be enormous advantages in this and new technology should play a particular part in ensuring consistency of approach across the country. There are, however, difficulties which need to be resolved. The major one is that it is only a minority of childcare inspectors that are currently expected to make routine and extensive use of new technology. This is a feature of their social services base. It has been characteristic of social services departments that new technology has been handled by the administrative staff and the professional fieldwork staff have not been encouraged – in some instances have been forbidden – to make direct use of it, particularly in the logging in of data. This is a reflection of the fact that there is a greater divide between professional and administrative staff than is the case in, for example, housing departments where it is common for some clerical staff to advance through the ranks to managerial grades with more professional responsibilities. The separation of the two spheres in the social services departments has led to administrative staff becoming defensive about their professional territory and keeping social workers out on the grounds they will only mess up the networks. It will take time to deal with the problems this will cause a service relying on direct use of the technology by the professional staff. Ironically, home working makes the use of new technology essential, but at the same time more difficult to develop, since staff will lack the kind of day-to-day colleague support that has helped some childcare inspection teams develop their practice in this respect.

There are other issues relating to IT. OFSTED want to regulate in as transparent a way as possible. I am all in favour of that. However, the sometimes excessive secrecy in social services departments does have its roots in real concerns about confidentiality and it will be necessary to set up systems that clearly separate out information on providers that should be public from information that should not. (Many of the databases currently used by childcare inspection teams are not set up properly to do this because it was assumed information would be kept in-house and this has created practical problems in cooperation with local children's information services.) There are also some childminders who will not want their details available on the Internet or any other public information system for a variety of reasons, including their concerns that their current addresses are not made known to people who might constitute some kind of threat to them. There are some services on the registers at present that are attached to residential units for women and children escaping domestic violence and care will need to be taken with the availability of information in this instance. New technology is the one issue on which OFSTED began practical work at an early date. They saw the need to do this and felt familiar with that aspect of operations. As they get more into it they may come across complications they had not anticipated, especially as local children's information services have been very critical of the Children's Information Services Development Project (CIS DP) which OFSTED see as the primary mechanism for transferring information from their register to parents and others.

The most problematic feature of the transfer was the way in which the human resources issues were not addressed with sufficient speed to allay the fears of the staff to be transferred. Perhaps because OFSTED was about to undertake major new responsibilities in the field of further education and had to invest in developing a working relationship with the Adult Learning Inspectorate, the transfer was scheduled for September 2001 rather than April 2002. Whatever the reasons for the decision, it is evident that a single date for the two transfers would have made it easier for many existing inspection staff to consider whether they wished to transfer to the Early Years Directorate or one of the regional care commissions. 'Synchronicity', as it was termed, was one of the demands frequently put forward during the passage of the Bill and it was unfortunate that it was ignored.

It is easy to be critical about the failure to produce information more quickly on service conditions issues, the imposition of the home-working model without discussion and the decision not to allow the national Care Standards Commission and the Early Years Directorate the same starting date. Against that, one has to set the clarity of the material on service conditions issues when it was produced and the fact that some of the uncertainties about such issues as the relative roles of local inspection teams and their regional offices came from a wish to listen to and learn from those already operating in the field before making decisions on some key issues. However, there does appear to have been a failure to appreciate the impact of some decisions and the delays in making other decisions on the staff awaiting transfer. The result was a significant slump in morale among those staff in the period from the summer of 2000 to January 2001 and it is difficult to escape the conclusion that some of those problems could have been prevented or at least alleviated.

Conclusion

It was, perhaps, inevitable that argument about the detail (of the new Day Care Standards or of the service conditions for staff in the Early Years Directorate) should have obscured to some extent the significance of the change in the regulation system that is now in process. It is a long way from the panic measure of 1948 to the changes in regulation that will be introduced in 2001 as part of a coherent national strategy on early years services. A lot of baggage has been accumulated along the way and it still threatens to encumber the work of the new regulatory regime. Part of that baggage is the continuing debate on the proper professional setting for early years work – the subject of my next chapter.

Chapter 3

Education, care and play

Introduction

The ways in which the care provided for young children, their educational development and their opportunities for play are inter-connected provide one of the major focal points of debate within the early years field. The debates as to what constitutes best practice in day-to-day work is, however, profoundly affected by differences in the institutional settings in which that work is conducted and the fact that different settings have some tendency to concentrate on one or the other of the three features of early work to the exclusion of the others. In this chapter it is the tension between different institutional settings on which I wish to concentrate. I believe an understanding of this issue helps us to address specific issues of quality in a more balanced way. It is certainly vital to the debate as to where the regulators of early years services should be organisationally located.

The decision to pass responsibility for the regulation of early years services to OFSTED formed part of a general transfer of this area of work to the DfEE and the LEAs. This represented a significant stage in a long process, a process of increasing integration of different services for young children. In a sense this was a return to the beginning. The earliest initiatives in early years services entailed no compartmentalisation. The ways in which things developed led, however, to a kind of specialisation in terms of health care and later social care, education and playwork, aspects of which were described briefly in Chapter 1. In the 1970s and 1980s this specialisation came to be seen by many as a source of difficulties. The pejorative term 'fragmentation' was used increasingly.

The long struggle against fragmentation

The creation of specialised systems is characteristic of modern industrialised societies and the existence of such systems brings in turn the development of increasingly complex networks to help people establish interconnectedness. The more individualised and less coherent social organisation becomes, the greater the demand for new mechanisms to enhance coherence in social policy.

When the growth in the demand for early years services in the last part of the 20th century made them an increasingly central concern for policy makers it was only natural that there should be a demand for greater coordination. Some felt certain that the continuing expansion of services would 'force re-examination of divided responsibility for day care and children below school age both at central and local government levels' (Goldschmied and Jackson 1994: 236).

It may have been natural that there should be a demand for greater coordination. It was not beyond question. Fragmentation had some advantages. It created opportunities for experiment. The development of the playgroup movement from the early 1960s, of adventure playgrounds in the 1960s and of community-based open access playschemes in the 1970s were all examples of this. It is also important to bear in mind that, while the *idea* of coherence in provision has immediate appeal, that does not in itself settle the question of the *basis* for it. Coherence can be based on the client group, the profession or on the organisational setting. The history of modern social policy is often one of moving from one basis for coherence to another. There is a real question as to why coherence should be focused around young children as such. Could the education and care systems and provision for recreation not each be seen as a coherent entity created for the benefit of children as much as of adults?

There is force in that argument. There is also the question of the boundaries of any coherent system. Even those who argue most passionately against fragmentation rarely suggest that the systems for protecting children against ill-health or abuse should be fully integrated with other early years services. The argument for coherence, although often based on notions of the need to respect 'the whole child', comes down in practice to questions of whether education or social work is to be the dominant profession in day-care services for children and whether the struggling profession of playwork can retain its own identity and agenda amid the tensions that arise. It may sound cynical to emphasise the place that an inter-professional dispute over influence has in what for many is a crusade. Unless that aspect of the situation is recognised, it will not be easy to resolve tensions nor to make pragmatic decisions on arrangements that will serve children's interests.

We need to clear that rubble out of the way as a preliminary to the more fundamental task defined by Moss, the exploration of 'whether there is an area of shared values in British society, on which base we can build a core area of agreement about quality' (Moss 1991: 12).

We are still some way from reaching that starting point. The weak commitment to integration of perspective evident in the new National Standards, the fact that the Curriculum Guidance for the Foundation Stage is presented in ways that suggest a relevance only to those providers that are eligible for a nursery grant, the continued reluctance of the Government to bring the United Kingdom (outside Ulster) into line with much of Europe and establish a distinct educational system for children from birth to their sixth birthday, the fear of the teaching unions that full integration of services for children under six will lead to cheaper services run by non-teaching staff at the expense of their members and of the children, the fact that vocational training in childcare and education is linked with health and social care rather than teaching – all these things are indications that the struggle for integration has some way to go.

This is hardly surprising since the fragmentation of early years services was well established in this country by the post-war period and the campaign against it started only about a quarter of a century ago.

In that campaign a leading role was played from the start by the Early Childhood Unit of the National Children's Bureau. The need for better coordination of services was also one of the key demands of the National Childcare Campaign (now the Day Care Trust) when it was set up in the early 1980s. Margaret Clark's 1987 report to the DES on current research on provision for the under-fives gave some indications of the need for better coordination. Within a few years this had become a more dominant theme in the literature. David (1994) edited a collection of articles on *Working Together for Young Children*. Another reader edited by Pugh (1996) on *Contemporary Issues in the Early Years* was sub-titled *Working Collaboratively for Children*. Hope was seen in the emphasis on the coordination and planning required of statutory services in the section 19 reviews required by the Children Act. It was also seen in the creation of several 'educare centres' following a variety of models, such as The Hillfields Nursery Centre (in Coventry), the Mosborough Under Fives Service (in Sheffield) and, probably most famous of all, the Pen Green Nursery Centre (in Corby). Following the example of Strathclyde. a number of local authorities, mainly in London and the industrial north of England, began to set up what were called 'integrated young children's services' within education departments. The number escalated in the period after the introduction of the National Childcare Strategy. At every level from that of the neighbourhood, to that of the local authority and on to the national level there was a slow but definite movement from fragmentation to greater collaboration and on through systematic coordination to full integration of services. And wherever this happened it was always the education system that was seen to take the primary role. Goldschmied and Jackson were voicing a view that was well on its way to becoming an orthodoxy when they wrote that 'The logical solution ... is to transfer services for the under-fives to the education departments' (Goldschmied and Jackson 1994: 36).

The picture from abroad

It was also part of that orthodoxy to claim that this was a pattern well established in other parts of the developed world and was an example worthy of imitation. This was not necessarily the case for two reasons.

One is that, as Cooper *et al.* (1995) say in their excellent book comparing child protection and family support systems in France and the UK, the principal advantage of looking at foreign models is that they remind us that things do not have to be done as we have always done them here (p. 131). Even if foreign systems are judged to be better than our own, they cannot simply be adopted. Social policy grows out of the culture of a nation and to import a foreign model without radical re-design is to risk a transplantation that will not 'take'. The early years services in some other European countries may be judged to be better than ours. It does not follow that we can simply do as they do without problems.

The second reason is that the picture from abroad is more complicated than some advocates of integration suggest. Among the Anglo-Saxon countries New Zealand approximates to the model it is suggested the UK should follow, but the USA does not. In the rest of the European Union the picture is also mixed. Spain and Sweden have systems that are well integrated and fall within the general system of education and it is these two countries that are most often cited in the anti-fragmentation literature. On the other hand, Austria, Denmark, Finland, Germany and Ireland have systems that are integrated but within the social services sphere. Belgium, Italy and the Netherlands have systems for under-threes that fall within the sphere of social services and for children aged two to six that come within the broader educational system. (It would be interesting to know more about how the overlap in the third year works out for children and their parents.) France, Greece, Luxembourg and Portugal have systems just as fragmented as our own. Greece is currently in a situation of transition and may move to a more integrated system. In France, where concerns over health played as central a role in the development of early years services as they did in this country, the transition from pre-school care to the education system is seen by many as problematic (Norvez 1990: 393–439).

It also has to be kept in mind that in countries with more federal structures than the UK, the share of responsibility between provinces or regions, on the one hand, and the federal government, on the other, may be more significant than the division of responsibility between education and social services. A further complication is that the boundaries of the social services are not necessarily seen as they are in this country. Terms which may be translated as 'educator' ('Erzieherin', the common term for school teacher, in Germany; 'éducateur' in Luxembourg) are employed to describe staff outside of the teaching profession. In Sweden the term is even used to describe a playworker, called a 'fritidspedagog' (free-time educator).

It may well be that New Zealand and Spain and Sweden have it right and the rest of us need to learn from them, but it cannot be argued (as it is sometimes implied) that Britain's failure to establish an integrated system led by education puts us out of step with everyone else.

Education as the institutional setting for early years work

The case for making education services the primary institutional setting for early years work rests on two types of assertion.

One is based on the growing body of research evidence that children are learning from the earliest possible stage (even in the womb) and can be assisted or impeded in that learning process by their surroundings. If child development is seen in terms of learning and education as well as a natural process of physical growth, then it may seem logical that the institutions that have responsibility for schooling should have responsibility for early years services as well since 'children's experience before the age of three is, for better or worse, just as much part of their education as anything that happens in schools' (Goldschmied and Jackson 1994: 237). There is a certain sliding from consideration of general principles to institutional arrangements in this kind of assertion. It fails to take into account that both early years services and the school system could be seen as reflections of the need for constant growth and re-learning in a complex and changing society. If learning takes place or should take place every-where, then either the teaching profession takes on responsibility for the world (which would change its nature) or else it accepts responsibility for a discrete area which might not include early years services.

The second type of assertion is that, as education is a service available to all children, it provides the kind of universal framework that early years services need. It is in itself an emblem against fragmentation. Again, there is a slide from general principles to conclusions about institutional arrangements. There are other universal services, health services in particular. The fact that there is a school system designed to serve the entire community does not automatically make education the only universal frame-work within which integrated early years services might flourish. However, the real basis for this second assertion is the contrast with social services seen as focused on the most disadvantaged and having, as a result, a stigmatised image, so I will deal with it at greater length in the next section.

What is probably true is that there is a much more solid basis of professional competence and confidence in education than in social services for taking on respons-ibility for early years. Given the talk there often is of a crisis in education, it might seem strange to speak of teachers having confidence in their ability, but there appears to be a different feel to early years teaching than there is to some other parts of the profes-sion. Certainly, the authors of a report on a project based in Leeds University, which involved people from a range of early years agencies, noted among the practitioner participants in the project some clear differences in this respect between teachers and others. While those that were not from the teaching profession often expressed lack of confidence about their ability to help children learn and confessed their unfamil-iarity with such terms as 'curriculum', the authors say that 'during the project we never heard those with backgrounds in educational services apologise for their lack of knowledge and understanding of children's physical and emotional needs' (Anning and Edwards 1999: 81). This is not a recent phenomenon. A quarter of a century ago Boyle observed in relation to Scotland at least that: 'Unlike nursery school staff, who are convinced of the positive value of their work, nursery staff have no great confi-dence in theirs. And the gloom is a breeding ground for a faulty service' (cited in Makins 1997: 2).

It might be questioned how far that self-confidence is justified. Writing in the early 1990s, Curtis claimed that for some teachers at least 'the requirements of the Council for the Accreditation of Teacher Education (CATE) will have prevented them from spending substantial periods of time working with and studying about children aged 3–5 years', and added: 'Whatever course they followed it is unlikely that they will have much knowledge of children from birth to 3 years' (Curtis 1994: 162). That criticism remains valid for the original professional training of many teachers, but of course a great deal has happened in the few years since Curtis made it. Changes in professional training may be less important in terms of confidence than the role given to education services in the National Childcare Strategy.

It might also be questioned whether there is confidence in the capacity of the teaching profession to take the leading role in early years services among the general public and among parents in particular. Very little is really known about parents' attitudes or understanding in relation to this issue. There is a widespread belief that parents are anxious to get their children into mainstream schooling as soon as possible, something that implies confidence in the education system at least at an early stage. However, there is little support for this view in the survey evidence gathered for the DfEE report *Tomorrow's Children* (DfEE 1999, para.121). If there is a pressure to get children into mainstream schools, it may be that parents are anxious to secure places for their children in particular schools and are, therefore, seeking them as early as possible for that reason rather than as an expression of confidence in the school system as such. Nevertheless, there is a good deal of anecdotal evidence of greater respect for teachers than other early years professionals among parents and this suggests hypotheses that could be both further tested and refined by research.

The literature, dominated as it is by figures from an educational background, does rather take for granted that integration means integration within the education system and this approach has been adopted by the present government. There is, nevertheless, opposition to this idea. It may be expressed in grumblings in corners more than in the published literature, but it is there and the August 1999 announcement about the transfer of regulation of early years services to OFSTED helped to focus minds.

There are a number of inter-woven strands to this hostility.

One is the notion that early years services should be essentially an extension of the nuclear family, whereas schools are seen as part of the wider world. Indeed, the advantages of nannies and childminders in the eyes of many are that they replicate in some senses the parent/child relationship in a home setting, while community playgroups and pre-schools still depend to a large extent on parent volunteers. This is not just a British attitude. It is reflected in many of the terms used across Europe. The French word 'crèche' (meaning originally 'cradle') is used in English, Portuguese and Dutch. Similarly, nurseries for children aged nought to three are called 'escoles bressol' ('cradle schools') in Catalan. The French term for nursery, 'école maternelle' (literally 'mother school'), is similarly indicative, as is the term 'day mother' ('Tagesmutter' 'dagmamma' 'madre de dia') for childminders in Austria, Germany, Sweden and Spain. In France the notion that childcare is an extension of motherhood has been carefully researched by Bloch and Buisson (1998). The view that day care for young children should be more like home the younger they are is reflected not just in the phraseology used, but in the emphasis on child:staff ratios.

A second strand relates to a view of OFSTED itself as a controlling body committed to a return to more traditional approaches in education. Even those who approve of this in secondary education may have reservations about such an approach to the care and education of very young children. Hence there was a spate of cartoons in the aftermath of the August 1999 announcement that suggested that OFSTED would behave quite inappropriately as the regulator of early years services. There was the practitioner who had to break the news to a distressed mother that Tommy had 'failed finger painting'. There was the OFSTED inspector asking the childminder about a baby in a pram whether he was up to long division yet? It would presumably come as a surprise to those who voiced this sort of sarcasm that it was OFSTED itself in one of its early reports that expressed concern about failures to understand the importance of play as a tool for learning in primary schools (OFSTED 1993).

A third strand is the identification of education with 'formal' approaches to education. There are some problems with this issue, mainly those associated with the fact that the very term 'formal education' is in practice defined differently by different people. A modest piece of research on the understanding of terms commonly used in the early years field that was conducted recently among experienced practitioners in Sheffield showed a higher level of discrepancy in the understanding of the term 'formal education' than almost any other covered. However, there is a difficulty that is one of more than mere semantics. An unintended effect of the funding regime for pre-school education now in place is that an increasing number of children are being brought into the maintained school sector before their fourth birthday. There are widespread fears that this is leading to a more academic curriculum than is desirable, partly because of the previous experience of teachers taking on such classes, partly because the staffing levels do not facilitate the approaches to activity that would be found in the better day nurseries. Concern over this issue was taken up by a Select Committee in Parliament in 2001. Publicity was given in the media at the same time to criticisms made by Kathy Sylva that 'in 25 years we have moved from no curriculum to an overly academic curriculum' (Sylva 2001). There is a view that bringing regulation of pre-school care within the ambit of education will encourage rather than discourage moves to more formal types of education.

What is missed by many of those that are afraid of situating primary responsibility for early years services in education is that the most sustained and detailed criticism of 'formality' has come from the teaching profession itself. Educationists played a leading role in persuading the Rumbold Committee not to impose a version of the National Curriculum on pre-school children (Rumbold 1990). It is educationists that have voiced opposition to pressures appearing in reception classes and in services for even young children as a result of the National Literacy and Numeracy Strategies (e.g. Anning and Edwards 1999: 85). It is educationists that have shaped the more informal approach in the Curriculum Guidance for the Foundation Stage.

This opposition is based on a number of considerations. There is the research evidence that programmes focused on promoting intellectual development are associated with more aggressive behaviour (Clarke-Stewart 1991: 54). There are the findings of the Oxford Team (Sylva cited in David and Nurse 1999). There have even been reservations expressed about the much-praised High Scope programme on the grounds that formally structured approaches of that kind may be introduced without the full initiation of parents required for their complete success (Sylva *et al.* 1986). The whole issue has been re-visited recently by Blenkin and Kelly (2000) in an article that points to the poor educational consequences of an over-emphasis on cognitive development in young children.

However, it is not detailed observations from research that fuel the drive against 'formality' so much as our general understanding of how children develop and learn. There is passion as well as intellectual appreciation in the way that many of the best known texts approach this issue.

Gardner, is content to observe:

> The years from birth to between seven and ten years form the *intuitive* or informal stage of learning, where processes *within* the individual play a key role in determining the forms of understanding accessible to children *without formal instruction.* (Cited Gura 1996: 143)

David and Nurse however protest vehemently against a formal curriculum that would make childhood

> less playful, less celebrated, less creative, less romantic, more pressurised, more serious, more confined, more directed. (David and Nurse 1999: 169)

Of course, the fear may be that voices such as these, though admirable, perhaps even typical, of experienced early years teachers, will be drowned in a push towards greater formality coming from Government. This is not inevitable. All the statements coming from ministers of the present Government have indicated a readiness to accept the importance of play and all that that implies in early years education. However, a number of considerations, including, probably, reluctance to offend the teaching unions, have prevented them from moving as firmly as some would like from statements of principle to institutional change (in particular to the creation of a system for children under six that is in some way separate from the main school system). This whole area remains a battleground, but one where early years specialists in the teaching profession have tended to agree rather than disagree with others in the pre-school field.

There remains, nonetheless, an anxiety that teachers have a narrow range of concerns, that their training and professional focus on work within the educational setting leave them ill-equipped to understand the whole lives of children and, therefore, make education an inappropriate setting for early years services in general and their regulation in particular. 'OFSTED needs to put children first', was the head-line over one letter in the social work journal *Community Care* (7–13 October 1999, 1293). What reasons were there for thinking that it would not? The same letter asserted that 'inspections should be broader based and not led or constructed by educationalists'. Another letter in the same issue spoke (on behalf of the Association of Directors of Social Services) of the need 'for children to be seen as children with a full range of educational, social, emotional and care needs' – again implying that educationists in general and OFSTED in particular could not be trusted to under-stand this.

Little of this kind of assertion was based on a critical account of what either teachers or OFSTED were doing. It was based rather on an assertion that the social work profession had a broader understanding of the needs of children than teachers did. So what is the basis for that assertion?

Social services as the institutional setting for early years work

As was said in the previous chapter, there was a widespread assumption among leaders of the social work profession that regulation of early years services would pass to the Care Commission along with other services when it was established in 2002. Even after the August 1999 announcement they did not immediately give up hope of persuading the Government to see things their way. The Association of Directors of Social Services called for a reversal of the decision and the British Association of Social Workers expressed concern about 'the possible risks children may face' as a result of it (Herbert 1999).

Yet only a week later the tone had changed. The demand being expressed in the social work press was no longer for responsibility to go to the Care Commission but rather that OFSTED should adopt approaches that adequately reflected the full range of the regulatory task and also 'draw on the talent that's already available' recruiting as many of the existing inspectorial staff as possible to the new agency (Valios 1999).

In spite of the heat generated in the short term, the attempt to change the Government's mind never really got anywhere. There was something symptomatic about this. While many, probably a majority, of the staff directly involved in the work were at home in the social services departments and were thinking in terms of transfer to the Care Commission, this was not an important issue for most leaders of the social work profession except in so far as it was a significant indication of a possible coming break-up of the social services departments themselves.

The risk of such a break-up was a live issue at the time and has remained so. Proposals from the NHS Confederation for new arrangements for community care of adults with a variety of difficulties threatened in the eyes of many an NHS take-over. The Government's plans for expansion of the Sure Start programme seemed to herald a complete loss of confidence in the ability of social services departments to take the lead in family support. Fears were expressed that social services departments were missing out in the development of regeneration programmes (Rickford *et al.* 2000).

This development was entirely predictable. The rug was pulled from under the feet of the social services departments in the early 1990s when they were divided up into quite separate sections dealing with adult clients of various kinds and children and between commissioning and providing services. The abandonment of the generic approach which had characterised the social services departments in the early 1970s robbed them of the justification for their existence. At the same time it became clear to many social workers that the professionalism of their activity did not need to rest upon a particular type of local authority department. It was a measure of the quality of leadership in the departments at the time that so few seemed to appreciate where things were going and spoke of the increasing internal fragmentation of the departments as a triumph.

As the majority of social workers began to reconcile themselves to the demise of the vision that had led to the creation of the social services departments, the loss of early years regulation and the direct delivery of day-care services came to seem an increasingly unimportant part of a larger scenario.

This only served to reflect the insignificant part that early years services had in the departments. There were, of course, many examples of excellent work undertaken by staff in field social work and in children's day care. The whole sphere of early years is one that tends to attract a particular degree of commitment. However, people had to take initiatives against a backdrop that was often one of indifference and they did not always find it easy to establish effective collaborative relationships with colleagues in other statutory agencies or in the voluntary sector or keep in touch with current thinking. Where specialist fieldwork posts had been created (in both regulation and advisory/support services) these were often seen as ripe for asset stripping as the funding problems of the departments increased.

The questionable future of the departments and the marginal role that early years services have had within them both have a bearing on any claim that the social services sphere presents the best institutional setting for early years services in general or regulation in particular.

It is useful to take the case of direct provision first since it is only when they are in close contact with such services that regulatory services can really flourish.

It was extremely rare – even in the late 1980s when the demand for childcare began to escalate – for social services departments to commit themselves to local strategies for the development of childcare services. The 'lack of resources' cannot be blamed for this, although it did not help. The so-called 'integrated' young children's services that were established in several education departments in the early 1990s all developed such strategies. They may have found it difficult to achieve as much as they wished because of lack of funds, but they were reasonably clear on what they wanted to achieve, what the priorities were and on the importance of seizing such opportunities (European Union funding, the Government's Challenge Fund, etc.) as were available.

Day-care services for young children were seen in terms of 'resources' for field social workers. This often gave rise to examples of dedicated and imaginative working by social workers that kept alive the notions of preventive work and family support. However, even at its best this kind of operation represented a restricted view of children's day care and the best was far from universal. The Social Services Inspectorate has been among those criticising a lack of proper communication and cooperation between fieldwork services, providers and childcare inspectors when children are placed in day care as means of assisting a family to deal more effectively with their problems (Social Services Inspectorate 2000, para. 7.11).

Two things arose from the notion that day care was a resource to be used by social workers with families in difficulty. The most obvious one was that the service was stigmatised in the eyes of users. Goldschmied and Jackson (1994) speak of the image of social services day nurseries as 'a service offered only to the most disadvantaged children' (p. 267). Whalley (1994) says that 'Day nurseries are held back from becoming relevant, accessible and exciting services by their historical association with child abuse and neglect' (p. 155). When plans were going ahead in the early 1980s for a combined education and social services pre-school provision in the south-east of Sheffield, parents were anxious to know that it was education that would play the leading role so that they could feel free to send their children without stigma.

Even more important than the stigma was the impact on the services themselves. In a provision that is truly centred on the needs of children, therapeutic objectives can have a natural and effective place. This is a lesson often lost on day-care services in the social services departments where, as Jackson observed, day care is 'on the fringes of the "looked after" system' and 'There is a tendency for social workers to hand over to the nursery and reduce contact with the parents instead of planning together how they can support and help the child and family and at the same time acknowledge their separate contributions and responsibilities' (Jackson 1994: 129). In this context there is nothing surprising in what Penn (1997) found in her examination of a number of English nurseries – a lack of commitment to training (p. 43), a failure to keep abreast of theoretical development (pp. 120–27), a failure to offer 'opportunities for fun, games, cooperation, secrecy, exploration, movement, exertion or challenge or even fresh air' (pp. 131–2), a reinforcement rather than solution to the weaknesses of the families from which the children came (p. 132). What is remarkable is that a number of day nursery principals were able to develop new ways of working that were more supportive to both parents and children. It is clear from Makins' 1997 survey of some of the more innovative projects that these were often exceptions in the local system, rarely used as models for development elsewhere in the same local authorities because of their expense and retained because of support from parents – flagships without fleets.

The poor record of social services departments with their own direct provision or use of the independent sector must cast doubt on the claim that the social services sector provides a solid base for regulation. The assertions that were made in the immediate aftermath of the August 1999 announcement were largely a knee-jerk response to a significant loss of empire that might signal worse to come. However, it is worth looking at what was said. The case for keeping responsibility for regulation in the social services sector was based on two types of assertion.

The first was rather narrow in focus. It was that it was only if social workers remained in control that proper attention was likely to be focused on child protection issues in children's day care. This was a primary theme in the response of the spokesperson of the Association of Directors of Social Services to the August 1999 announcement. The British Association of Social Workers saw risk assessment as a role for which managers in OFSTED were unlikely to have 'the proper training and qualifications'. It was not clear whether 'risk assessment' here was meant to cover accidental as well as deliberate harm. If that were the case, it could be argued that social services staff have rarely had the qualifications to make the kinds of risk assessments that environmental health officers and others undertake and the development of childcare inspection teams in that respect has been patchy and dependent on the support of colleagues in other regulatory services. Thus, if there is any strength to the argument it must rest on the issue of child protection. Even before the August 1999 announcement it was common to hear senior managers in social services departments express concern that attention to child protection would not be lost if Children Act inspectors were transferred to the 'integrated' young children's services that many local authorities sought to establish. In response to pressure from social services Directors, OFSTED agreed a 'protocol' governing the connections the Early Years Directorate would have with child protection services. The evidence that this was produced in response to pressure is that it appeared before decisions were made on the division of responsibility between regional offices and local inspection teams, an issue of crucial importance if the protocol is to mean anything in practical terms.

And yet it does seem rather odd to claim that social work needs a particular connection with early years day care and education in a way that it does not with the mainstream schools system and other areas of life affecting children directly. Young children may be particularly vulnerable in some ways, but so are older children with disabilities. There has been good and less good practice in the social services departments in the period since implementation of Part X of the Children Act, but it is far from clear that the opportunities for particular collaboration between child protection and early years regulation services have been used universally in effective and innovative ways. The issue is not whether child protection is or is not a key issue. Nor is it whether or not early years regulators should participate actively in work to protect children in particular cases and in groundwork initiatives. (It was one of my colleagues in the Under Eights Team in Sheffield that took the leading role in developing a user-friendly code of conduct for people working with children, whether or not in settings registered under Part X. This code was published under the auspices of the area child Protection Committee. There have been other initiatives of that kind throughout the country.) The question is whether social services needs to retain responsibility for regulation to ensure that proper attention is paid to child protection. I have never seen a detailed case made for that proposition.

The other kind of assertion is that social services staff take a broader view of children and their needs than do educationists. Writing as someone whose own background is in social services rather than education, I have to say that seems to me to be arrogant and bigoted nonsense; yet it was often put forward in the summer of 1999.

It is difficult to see the basis on which the assertion is made. Among field and residential social workers, nursery nursing staff, teachers and playworkers there are people who show considerable skill in analysing the needs of young children and responding to them and their parents appropriately. And there are others who do less well or even badly. To a greater extent than is comfortable, practice depends on their individual experiences and personality. Both teaching and social work have important deficits in many of their professional training programmes in relation to child development. Where the subject is approached it is often from a circumscribed perspective, bound by respect for laboratory procedures rather than other approaches and taking too often for granted expectations in Anglo-Saxon society that do not exist in the same way elsewhere (Woodhead *et al.* 1998).

However, when one examines the theoretical literature and the organisation of practice in the two professions, a much more differentiated picture emerges.

The literature of early years education is very clearly focused on the needs of the whole child in ways that relate directly to practice. Teaching itself entails constant contact with children. Proper reflection on that experience by the individual practitioner or the theoretician leads, not quite inevitably but very frequently, to comprehensive understanding of the needs of children.

In the literature of social work, on the other hand, there is nothing like the same focus on contact with the child. There are exceptions, such as Doyle's book on working with abused children. Even in that case it is notable that her focus is on work with children already identified as abused, that a good deal of the book is taken up with the issues of work with parents and carers, that there is much more on older children than on pre-school children and that she acknowledges that in her own practice '… I had concentrated on helping the parents. It was, after all, easier to communicate with fellow adults. Furthermore, I could largely dismiss the pain felt by children if I concentrated on the parents' needs' (Doyle 1990: x). When reference is made to interaction in day-to-day practice, the greatest emphasis is on collaboration with fellow professionals, the next priority is an understanding of the parents and consideration of how to conduct direct contact with children comes a poor third. This is a reflection of the status system within social services in the UK in comparison with the situation in many other European countries. It is field social workers that have status and prestige within the social services sector in the UK, whereas in many other developed countries status goes to residential and day-care workers who are seen as having a better opportunity to analyse the child and respond directly to her needs. The consequence of this has been since the 1950s an emphasis in the UK on social diagnosis based on verbal interaction which in turn gives higher priority to understanding the perceptions and behaviour of the adults involved in any situation. Where early years day-care staff and trainers have entered into dialogue with social workers they have often been shocked by their poor understanding of child development and limited ability to interact with children productively. In cases where young children have died at the hands of parents or other carers in spite of the involvement of social workers, the failure of the social worker to engage directly with the child has often been a crucial factor. The case of Anna Climbie seems likely to join the list when we have the report of the statutory enquiry set up by the Health Secretary in January 2001. The plain fact is that if people have not had the personal strengths to develop skills in communicating with young children by themselves, the social services departments and the social work training courses have often failed to help them make good that deficit.

Therefore I would not consider the transfer of early years regulation to the Care Commission to have ever been a viable alternative. Such a move would have kept the activity within the narrower perspectives that social work has adopted and by weakening the link with field social workers and others in the social services departments themselves would have undermined the one aspect of working in those departments that did often lead to effective work by committed individuals.

That is a matter of the situation as it has emerged in history. There was nothing inevitable about it. A year before the planned date of transfer, the Social Services Inspectorate produced their report on eight childcare inspection teams which highlighted the failure in many places to integrate the work of regulation with developing childcare and education strategies (SSI 2000). Their criticism of practice to date adds some strength to the argument I have made here. Coming as it does from a key part of the social services establishment, it demonstrates clearly that things need not have been that way. But by then it was too late. The usefulness of the report is overshadowed by the fact that it has something of the deathbed conversion about it.

Playwork as the institutional setting for early years work

There is another setting that could be considered and that is playwork, that is to say activity designed to foster and facilitate play outside educational settings in the context of after-school clubs, holiday playschemes, adventure playgrounds and services of that kind.

This is something that should not be overlooked because playwork staff, especially those within leisure services departments, bring a particular and essential focus to early years work. Playworkers have their own take on the role and purposes of play for children in the later primary age group for whom there is wider agreement that more formal approaches to education are appropriate. Thus they offer a different perspective on the question of the ways in which play relates to care and education. Since they are dealing with children who have for the most part achieved many basic skills, they have an approach to risk assessment and an appreciation of adventure that can serve as a corrective to the one-sided focus on safety coming from the health/care tradition in early years (Melville 1997). Playwork is also the only sector of early years work to date where men are found in any numbers and that experience is one demanding attention. The development and implementation of a local play policy has been a priority for many of the local partnerships. Playworkers bring more than their special area of expertise to the work of partnerships or the planning of regulation. It is also important that the legislative and political background to their work (from the Recreation Ground Act 1859 through the Physical Training and Recreation Act 1937 to more recent government initiatives) has been about promotion of activity rather than regulation in response to traumatic incidents. Factors such as these make it essential that playwork is an integral part of any early years strategy.

That having been said, it should be clear that because leisure services departments are smaller than education and social services departments and because they do not link in the same way to major national agencies, they do not have the institutional strength and capacity to take a leading role. The fact that the attention of the local partnerships and of early years regulation is focused more on the pre-school years offers a reason to seek greater influence for playworkers, but it would be eccentric to make their role the leading one in the field. Indeed, the risk is that playworkers will be marginalised in the early years sphere and that, feeling marginalised, they will link more closely to other staff engaged in recreation for older children and adults at the expense of work with the rest of the early years scene.

A separate set of professional institutions for early years work?

There is an alternative to giving responsibility to social services or to education or to any other existing set of institutions. That alternative would be to create an entirely separate set of institutional arrangements specifically for early years work. As the long struggle against fragmentation works its way slowly towards a successful conclusion, this might seem the logical outcome. Already the DfEE and others have adopted the practice of referring to 'practitioners' in early years work rather than to particular professional groups or lists of such groups. Moss (2000: 13) asks:

> Why are we so reluctant to explore the possibility of new types of early childhood workers, to replace 'childcare' workers and 'teachers' – perhaps pedagogues or early years teachers, or perhaps something else quite different?

The proposal that there should be separate institutional arrangements (including arrangements for inspection and regulation) developed for work with the under sixes has some logic to it. On the other hand, it is easy to see why the Government has taken a more pragmatic approach and insisted that good practice in early years work is not dependent on major institutional reform, that such re-organisation might, indeed, prove a distraction from getting on with the qualitative and quantitative development of services. It takes a major effort to establish a new and comprehensive set of institutional arrangements.

We have, after all, been here at least once already in the recent past. The history of community work in this country from the late 1960s to the early 1990s was be-devilled by conflict as to whether the activity needed its own set of professional institutions, a conflict that resulted in victory for none of the rival viewpoints and did much to impede the development of practice as a key element in regeneration.

The case for the Early Years Directorate

The case for establishing the Early Years Directorate is that the arrangement might as well be that. There was a strong case for retaining responsibility for regulation within local authorities. The Government has, however, decided to prioritise consistency and rightly believes that consistency is not easily compatible with the sort of variation that follows from local decision making on policy.

That decision falls well within a tradition of thinking about social policy in this country where there has always been a strong impulse in favour of territorial justice, that is to say the notion that people should be treated in essentially the same way by the machinery of the state wherever they happen to live. This may seem so obvious as to be unquestionable. Other countries, however, have given a higher priority to innovation and excellence at the price of fewer people receiving some kinds of service. If territorial justice (of which consistency is one aspect) is to be the overriding consideration, we will tend to have more fairness, but also more centralised decision making and bureaucracy (which everyone claims to hate) and less innovation and initiative. The consequence could be lower morale among staff delivering services and lower levels of approval for public services among users and the general public. Everything depends on which is seen as the overriding value. The Blair Government was committed to the idea of consistency and naturally chose to transfer regulation from local government to a national body.

If there is to be a national body, it cannot be located within social services or recreation or within a separate area of professional work labelled 'early years' which at best is in an early stage of development. If education is to be the setting for early years work in general, it makes sense to give responsibility to Her Majesty's Chief Inspector rather than set up a new national body from scratch. However, the scale of the regulatory work that needs to be undertaken does suggest that OFSTED cannot simply undertake the work within its present structures, but needs to establish a distinct structure within its overall organisation. Whatever the reservations many people have about giving responsibility for regulation in this sphere to a new arm of OFSTED, it is difficult to think of a practical alternative once the decision had been made on grounds of prioritising consistency to take responsibility away from local government.

'It might as well be OFSTED' is neither the ringing endorsement for which some might hope nor the rousing condemnation others want to hear. It does appear to be the best possible reflection of the stage of development we have reached. Whether the logic of development within this country or increasing pressure to conform to other European models will change that situation is something that remains to be seen.

Chapter 4

Regulation, development and quality assurance

Introduction

The establishment of the Early Years Directorate will create not just an opportunity but the need to re-negotiate the relationship between providers and regulators.

The differences of approach between local authorities make it impossible to retain many of the existing features of the regulatory system without sacrificing the move towards consistency that provides the justification of the change. The very fact of creating a national system will change the relationship with providers. There will not be the same opportunities to influence the ways in which the childcare inspectors operate through the local democratic process. The decision to have regional offices rather than offices within each partnership area will reduce the opportunities for less formal exchange and interaction.

Many of the statements from political and official sources in London have suggested that the Early Years Directorate will regulate and it will be for local partnerships to support and develop. It is recognised that some existing local authority childcare inspection teams engage in development and support as well as regulation and that, therefore, some existing staff may be retained in their local education departments as advisors, capacity-building staff, development workers or whatever to meet the requirements of section 79V of the Care Standards Act. The detailed regulations relating to that section are due to be issued in the spring of 2001 as are the requirements made by the DfEE of early years partnerships in relation to recruitment, training and quality assurance for the period 2001–4 which provide a framework. The distinction between regulation and support sometimes appeared to be seen as straightforward – such that it could be reflected easily in organisational arrangements and clear definition of role.

The issue seems to me more problematic than that. It is one of the strengths of the SSI (2000) report that it recognises much of that complexity.

The different forms of development

Part of that complexity rests in the fact that the word 'development' is often used to mean quite different things in this context.

There is the development of the regulatory regime itself. Few would dispute that all childcare inspectors should have the opportunity to influence guidelines and procedures, although that influence is likely to be weaker with a large workforce operating across the whole of the country than it was in those local authorities that had small specialist teams working in this field.

Then there is the development of the work of the local childcare partnerships. OFSTED has committed itself to giving a significant role to senior childcare inspectors (the local team leaders) in this work, although they also appear to have underestimated the extent to which some local authority childcare inspection teams had contributed to it or how much investment might be needed to supplement the work of the Children's Information Service Development Project (CIS DP) which is intended to be the primary information source for local children's information services.

A third form of development work is in relation to the promotion of quality within partnerships as a particular aspect of the local plans. The Early Years Directorate will have to determine the priority it wishes its basic grade staff to give to this kind of work. Failure to allow for it properly would rob local partnerships of an important source of ideas and information. Even more important is the question of the impact on inspectors of engaging in this kind of work which seems to me essential if they are to keep properly abreast of the latest thinking in the field (especially at local level) and to avoid the development of a merely bureaucratic mentality that is likely to come from an unremitting treadmill routine of formal assessments.

There may well be differences of opinion about the extent to which childcare inspectors should be engaged in these three forms of development. (The initial proposals on pay scales imply a more limited involvement than some of the staff involved had hoped to see.) However, there is less likely to be controversy over the principle that there should be some involvement. There is also likely to be little controversy over the idea that the Early Years Directorate should not be engaged in development work with individual providers intended to help them improve the quality of their performance or their overall efficiency and viability as organisations. Section 79V of the Care Standards Act clearly leaves responsibility for that area of work with the local authorities.

The most problematic aspect of this issue is the question of whether regulation can be conducted in a form that is usually supportive. It is a fundamental proposition of this book that it can be. For others this is unacceptable. Some of those in the social services departments that were fiercest in their denunciation of the transfer to OFSTED here, ironically, find themselves in agreement with some of the strongest advocates of the change. The idea of conducting regulation in an essentially supportive manner seems impossible to both those who see the essential, almost exclusive, task of regulation in terms of protecting children from harm and those who wish to distinguish organisationally, as well as theoretically, between inspection and support. I hope to demonstrate that the enforcement of the distinction is unhelpful.

Standards and quality

The Guidance issued to local authorities under the Children Act made it clear that the purpose of inspection was both 'to ensure that services are being provided to an acceptable standard' and 'to encourage day care providers and childminders to raise standards' (volume 2, para. 8.7). This combination of objectives has never been easy and it has been argued that confusion between the two has been the source of inconsistencies between local authorities. Some providers have always wanted childcare inspectors to restrict their role to ensuring minimum standards are being maintained and pressure in this direction has grown as provider networks have acquired an increasing number of development and advisory staff. Some have queried whether inspection reports should include recommendations as well as requirements to be met, saying that parents often fail to understand the distinction and may feel that an inspection report with a considerable number of recommendations must indicate a lower standard at the setting.

There was also pressure self-generated within childcare inspection teams themselves. The need to justify their own existence has sometimes led to a feeling that they must find problems whenever they inspect in order to demonstrate that they are doing something. This can lead to a hyper-critical approach and also to bald statements that a provider has failed to meet standards in situations where there has been something needing to be rectifying but the overall quality has been good. Anxieties arising from particular cases of abuse (the Shieldfield Nursery in Newcastle, the deaths of children in the care of childminders) have focused attention on the issue of whether childminders and those involved in group care are 'fit persons'. The concentration on vetting of owners, group care staff, childminders and their families has involved an immense amount of work that has distracted from attention to other issues. It has also often led to a culture in which the issue of quality could not be addressed. In practice, decisions as to whether anyone was a 'fit person' have been a form of negative vetting. People have been accepted as fit because there was no clear evidence to the contrary. (Changes in terminology in the Care Standards Act are designed to tackle this issue, but those changes will not in themselves produce a change in outlook and expectations among either providers or childcare inspectors.) In addition, issues of safety have been assessed in relation to standards that are in the most literal sense measurable rather than on the basis of comprehensive risk assessment.

Both providers and childcare inspectors feel a strong need to have their position clarified. It is, therefore, unsurprising that there should be some pressure to focus on the imposition of standards rather than the promotion of quality. 'Quality' is, after all, a rather slippery concept – more of a slogan than a concept. It is about values rather than procedures; about wanting the best for children rather than about settling for what will do. Some aspects of quality are not open to simple measurement. The quality of cooperation with parents or of attention to equal opportunities are obvious examples. And since it is about values, there is the question of whose values are to define quality. As Petrie (1994: 188–93) points out in the context of out-of-school care and play, the different stakeholders may wish to apply different criteria. Perhaps those who constructed the Guidance in volume 2 were being naive in expecting that inspection could be a means of promoting quality. The question is still open to debate as to whether the Early Years Directorate needs to focus on standards and the protection of children from harm rather than on quality whose promotion may be left to initiatives within the local partnerships.

There are reasons to doubt such a conclusion. Others have made the point before that there is no reason why 'minimum' standards should be low ones. It depends on the importance we attach to the experiences of children in early years provision. If we want the best possible for them, then minimum standards will have to be set high and that will also involve finding criteria for those areas where this is more complex. Perhaps more should be expected of both providers and childcare inspectors.

Then there is the fact that the distinction between standards and quality is far from absolute. There is, on the contrary, a high degree of correlation. If it is to be measured, quality must be defined in operational terms and a readiness to meet specific standards is evidence of a disposition to achieve a quality of care and education. The effort to be as good as possible is the best defence against failure to meet standards.

Finally, there is the fact that some balance of judgement is required. A provider who fails to meet standards in one particular respect, but offers a good service overall must be judged by the inspector in those terms. Some issues may require flexibility, not to be soft on providers but to enable them to provide a good service. For example, it is essential that there should be a minimum number of qualified people in the staff group. However, that minimum number need not be maintained everywhere at every moment. Arrangements for lunch times or brief periods at the beginning and end of the day that entail use of other staff not necessarily childcare qualified may provide opportunities for the qualified staff to have proper breaks or to engage in planning and work on record systems and thereby contribute to the overall quality of the setting. Similarly, it is important that in general age bands in rooms should not be so wide as to create difficulties for younger or less confident children, but excessive rigidity in this matter fails to take into account the fact that children do not develop in strict accordance with their age and the usefulness of some interaction between different age groups. (There is a risk at present that the DfEE's perception of its planning needs and the kind of statistical data it requires will lead to the imposition of unhelpful prescription on age bands in full day-care nurseries.) Overall judgement of the nature of a provision is an essential part of the process, as is proper assessment of risk in relation to health and safety issues.

It is easy to understand why some childcare inspectors have focused on the measurement of performance against specific standards, on the check list approach to inspection. To some extent it is a matter of people minding their own backs, but it is a short-sighted approach even in those terms. If racism or systematic abuse at a provision come to light after an inspection has taken place, no one is likely to be impressed by the fact that the childcare inspector who missed the signs of those problems did detect some minor infringement of the regulations on the control of substances hazardous to health.

Consistency and flexibility

The question of whether consistency or flexibility should prevail in early years regulation is key to the relationship between standards and quality. The moves to establish the Early Years Directorate and to develop a new set of national standards are based to a significant extent on the desire for consistency. Though these moves have come from central government, it is clear the primary pressure producing them has come from independent providers, especially in the commercial sector, who wish to see a 'level playing field' in order to manage their business planning. It makes particular sense for those companies working in several local authority areas to be able to produce operational packages that will be relevant wherever a particular setting is planned.

Yet at the same time, many of those pressing for consistency are likely to argue that childcare inspectors have been inflexible in the application of regulations in particular circumstances. In some cases this may be a plea for leniency because the provider is facing hard times, but often the argument will be made that proper provision for the children requires some flexibility in the application of guidelines.

It has to be emphasised from the start that there is a difference between 'letting people off' requirements because the inspector feels sorry for them and accepting that it is appropriate to adopt a measure of flexibility in the interests of the children. Moreover, flexibility is not necessarily an occasional departure from the rules. It is built into the very notion of quality. If those running a unit are trying to make it as good as possible, it is inevitable that they will focus on some particular aspect that seems important to them because they have thought things through for themselves. They may pride themselves on their recruitment and training of local people, on their cooperation with parents, on their imaginative use of outdoor play, on their innovative approach to laying the foundations of an understanding of science or on some other thing they feel they do particularly well. More fundamentally, they may adopt a particular approach to some aspect of their work that is not the conventional one. A good example of this is the internal organisational structure of a day-care provision. It is too easy for childcare inspectors to think in terms of hierarchical structures. Steiner schools and some community nurseries run successfully with much more democratic structures. The issue is whether there is or is not an effective organisation, not whether the organisation matches up to a common blueprint. The important thing is that some idiosyncrasy of approach is one of the marks of a well-run setting. One that meets all the standards but does nothing more would be defective because that complete commitment would be missing.

The notion that quality might be measured by some degree of deviance from standards rather than strict adherence to them is difficult for both providers and childcare inspectors. It requires self-confidence on either side before it will work. There are a number of instances in which this issue becomes acute. There are cases where strict safety standards seem to be breached because providers allow opportunities for children that entail calculated risk – adventure playgrounds or the use of some natural materials in Steiner nurseries are examples. There are services which operate with particular understandings of child development that do not fit exactly with the common models in mainstream pre-school education.

Of course, deviations such as these must be carefully considered. The provider must not fail to meet standards because meeting them would be too expensive or because the staff cannot be bothered. If real thought and commitment has gone into the arrangement that challenges some specific aspect of standards, then that will be apparent. Childcare inspectors may find this difficult, but it is the childcare inspector who is confident in the practice she brings with her from the type of direct service delivery with which she is most familiar who is most likely to be open-minded about alternative approaches.

Objectivity and detachment

Both enforcement of minimum standards and promotion of quality require objectivity on the part of the childcare inspector, but the checking of standards allows for procedures that appear at least to be more objective.

In its work in the inspection of schools, OFSTED has often been seen as taking objectivity to the point where support is seen as incompatible with objectivity. Even a relatively friendly commentator says:

> The evidence suggests that some continuous co-operation between a school willing and able to evaluate its own performance and an external 'agency' which is sympathetic in its response to the school's needs is most likely to be successful. An OFSTED inspection, reflecting as it does the sharp separation of inspection and advice, doesn't seem to fit the bill and may be counter-productive. We must find a more constructive balance between pressure and support. (Learmouth 1996: 58)

It is not yet clear whether similar issues will arise in the case of the Early Years Directorate. A point that can be made is that the situation in early years services is quite different from that in schools. We have had universal schooling for 130 years in this country and school structures recognisably similar to our own for much longer than that. There are many controversies around school organisation and curriculum but they take place in a context in which much is agreed. Even the 'free schools' of the 1960s and 1970s and earlier experiments in the 1920s and 1930s had points of similarity with the mainstream. Given that consistency, it may be reasonable to measure achievement in schools against national criteria. The fragmentation of the early years scene, on the other hand, make consistency and objectivity even more difficult to achieve in inspecting their services.

A fundamental question for the Early Years Directorate is whether the same childcare inspectors will be involved in all assessments made of a provider (initial registration, annual inspections and any necessary investigations) or whether each assessment would be allocated to a new member of staff to ensure objectivity.

The personal relationships that develop over time between an inspector and a provider can give rise to collusion, to a willingness on the inspector's part not to look too closely at some aspects of the provision. On the other hand, it is not clear that to assign each new assessment to a new member of staff is an adequate way of avoiding that problem. There could, for example, be a culture within a team of not expecting very much of the service a nursery offers to babies so that each individual worker would collude with each provider in accepting a low standard. While it may be less easy to demonstrate or guarantee, I would see the basis of avoiding collusion as being the professional commitment and integrity of the staff rather than any arrangement for task allocation. If childcare inspectors are committed to seeking the success of providers, this will entail tough-minded thinking and action in response to weaknesses rather than do anything to impede such an approach.

Competence in observation is an essential part of objectivity in inspection and investigation. There are several difficulties here, such as the complexity of what there is to observe, the artificiality of the inspection situation when people are trying to be at their best and are aware of being observed, the fact that what is being observed is a moment in time which may not be typical. While most childcare inspectors would say that the people are the most important thing, followed by the premises, with the paperwork in the third and final place, the time spent on each of these at inspection often suggests a reverse order of priorities. (Hopkins 2000: 110–18 makes a similar point about inspection of elderly people's homes). One reason for this is that the paperwork and the buildings stay still to be measured up, counted and recorded, whereas the interaction between the provider's staff and children or their parents is a continuously moving show. The fact that some things are easier to observe does not make it more important to do so. Making observations of activity and interaction that are as detailed and precise as possible is difficult. It is also difficult to make observation reflective, that is to say to take into account the inspector's own feelings and values, the possible impact of her presence and the fact that the observation is time-limited. That is why inspections under the Children Act have often been based on check lists and similar documents. At best these draw the inspector's attention to issues; they do little to help to form judgements on them and may actually inhibit such activity. Something designed to help give a shape to the noisy and disparate picture an early years provision often presents can become a straitjacket inhibiting more than the most superficial kind of observation. Failures of observation at routine inspections can create the foundation for incompetent investigation where the very specificity of the issue under investigation will prevent the use of general purpose check lists and the need for clarity as to what has been observed and what has been deduced is even more critical.

The form in which observations are put in their final recorded form are also crucial. Jargon in reports on registration assessments, inspections or investigations not only make it difficult for the provider to appreciate what is being said, they make it easier for the childcare inspector to avoid being clear about what she is trying to say in situations where she feels uncertain of her ground or is unwilling to face up to conflict. Similarly, excessive use of the passive voice in reports often confuses the nature of the evidence and is a good sign that the inspection itself may not have entailed as much critical thought as necessary.

Another aspect of report writing is the extent to which a coherent picture of the strengths and weaknesses of a provider are clearly outlined and related to each other. Most registration and inspection report formats issued under the Children Act are based on lists of issues to be considered. The modelling of the new national standards could easily lend itself to such an approach with 1 section for each of the 14 standards. This is probably the most useful starting point for a format, but it could lead to a situation where each standard is considered separately and neither the connections between them nor the overall judgement being made on the unit are clear. Again, an appearance of objectivity is attained without the most useful kind of judgement being made.

It is vital in all this to distinguish between objectivity on the one hand and detachment or distance on the other. Objectivity is not achieved through detachment (though that is a useful tactic in many situations); it comes through clarity about the evidence and value base from which judgements are derived.

If primary value is ascribed to detachment in the struggle for objectivity, then there can be little or no question of involving others in the process of assessment. Yet there is much to be gained by constructive engagement with providers, their staff, parents and the children themselves. The failure to make use of these opportunities is the major source of weakness in the detachment model of objectivity.

Involving providers and their staff in the process of assessment

There are a number of ways in which providers and their staff can be actively engaged in the process of inspection rather than being merely the objects of it.

The extent to which inspectors and providers can act in partnership needs to be clarified. Of course, the regulatory function means that it is always possible that the inspector will have to recommend refusal to accept applications from providers or propose that sanctions be taken against them. This is why inspectors can never be seen merely as consultants nor providers as customers of their service.

If it is wrong to avoid facing up to those factors, they should not be exaggerated. The law requires providers to allow inspectors entry. It does not oblige them to like the inspectors. However, no great harm is done if they do and there should at least be mutual respect. In 1998 when consultations were in progress about the proposed NVQ IV qualifications in nursery management and in inspection and advisory work, some were anxious that the qualification for inspectors should be at a higher level than that for nursery managers. How else could they exercise authority over them or justify doing so? But the relationship between manager and inspector is not the same as that between manager and more senior manager (though many whose experience has been in the heavily hierarchical setting of a social services department find that difficult to appreciate). The roles of inspector and unit manager are different, not necessarily at different levels. There should be no problem about accepting that managers or leaders of group care services may have greater professional experience and skills than those that inspect them. Inspectors have to deal with a wide variety of settings and are unlikely to be equally experienced in all of them. The development of thinking about early years services is now so intense that even an inspector with a good deal of experience in the past may find herself falling out of date in her thinking after a few years as a childcare inspector. The people working at a particular provision will also be expert in all sorts of considerations that are specific to their community, their clientele and their premises. Without surrendering the authority and responsibilities they have taken on, childcare inspectors must be prepared to learn from those they inspect. If they do not, then inspection will come to have a deadening and regressive impact.

That readiness to learn must include a readiness to consult providers on the assessment processes involved in regulation. In the period leading up to the implementation of Part X of the Children Act, all local authorities devised processes for conducting registration assessments, annual inspections and investigations as well as local regulations and guidelines. Most have revised these at least once since then. This process has normally involved staff in the regulatory service drafting guidelines and procedures and then consulting providers on them in a variety of ways. This was the standard and probably the simplest way of going about the business of consultation. It is easier for providers to comment on a draft document than to produce ideas out of the air. If it was the easiest, it was not necessarily the best. There were advantages when some services tried forms of inspection and then sought feedback. It could be argued that for the most part too much initiative in the design of processes and guidelines was retained by the inspection service and that there was often too little attempt to seek consensus on the basis of debate starting from general principles. The process of general consultation will become more difficult now that regulation is being taken from local authorities and handed over to a national agency. However representative organisations such as the NDNA, the PLA, the NCMA or Kids Clubs Network may be, the process of consulting providers through them is bound to involve individual providers less than the processes initiated by local childcare inspection teams have been.

This makes it all the more important that there is a measure of consultation with providers over assessments specific to themselves. Guidelines cannot be determined on the basis of a popular vote – or at least not one where providers are the only voters. But, if there is widespread reluctance among providers to accept a particular standard, then there is a real problem. The standard itself may need to be considered afresh. If those that devised it remain convinced of its validity after review, then ways have to be found to persuade providers of the case for it. Such persuasion is likely to be more effective than the mere exercise of authority which only encourages people to find means of evasion.

At the very least providers need to have clear information on how assessments will be conducted. Each side also needs to be aware of and attempt to take into account the difficulties the other will face in the process of assessment. Beyond the exchange of clear information there needs to be some consultation as to how the inspection or other form of assessment will take place. Providers should be asked whether the planned process of an inspection makes sense or whether some change would be advisable. On the other hand, the readiness of some childcare inspectors to arrange inspections at the convenience of providers has interfered with their ability to ensure that inspections are held annually and may in some instances have helped providers conceal aspects of their practice.

An important aspect of consultation over specific assessments is that they should include a measure of self-assessment by the provider. Most inspection processes entail seeking some written evidence from the provider (and the same is also true of registration and investigation). The information sought is sometimes confined to hard details. Providers should be invited to evaluate their own performance, to make action plans and to report on progress in implementing them. Self-evaluation is always difficult but eligible providers have some experience of this because of what is required of them in that capacity. Childminders and providers of smaller scale, community-based group childcare services may find it more onerous. This should not be the occasion for excessively critical comment by the childcare inspector about the provider, but neither is there any reason for ignoring failures to engage in self-evaluation. It is important that providers are helped to do this if they have difficulty – in the first instance by the inspector; and by support/advisory staff from the local authority or provider networks where that is available. The childcare inspector that makes her own evaluation without any reference to the difficulty a provider has had in cooperating through self-assessment is losing an opportunity to help in the development of a service.

Consultation is also possible at the point at which an assessment process is nearing its conclusion. The inspector's judgements and the requirements and recommendations that follow on from them should be tested out with the provision. This is often done with the manager, but should also, wherever possible, be done with the owner (or representatives of the owner, such as the members of a management committee) and the staff. 'This is how it seems to me. Does that seem fair to you?' is the sort of question that should be put back to the provision on all the major conclusions of the assessment, especially any that will lead to the imposition of new requirements or any demand backed by possible sanctions that existing requirements be met in full. 'Verbal feedback' at the end of inspections can be seen as a way of not leaving the provider and the staff on tenterhooks, waiting to see what the inspector will conclude. It should be much more a matter of testing the conclusions to which the inspector has come before they are placed on record and possibly become a matter of dispute. Similarly, there should be a real attempt to arrive at agreement on action plans and there should be joint approaches to those who may be able to provide further support whether in the setting or by providing access to training identified as needed.

There must be some balance of power in the relationship between provider and inspector. Engaged in the task of inspecting others, childcare inspectors themselves are often wary of having their own work observed. Yet if inspection is essential to guarantee that standards are met by providers, it should be an instrument for ensuring the continuing quality of the work of regulation. 'Who will inspect the inspectors?' is one of the questions the Early Years Directorate will have to face.

The traditional answer in the Children Act inspection teams (derived from received ideas within the social work profession) is that individual supervision of staff will provide inspection of the inspectors. That kind of activity is vital and it was important that OFSTED recognised it in developing the idea of team leading Senior Childcare inspectors in the new service. The weakness of such supervision is that the supervisor is almost entirely dependent on the inspector's own account of what is happening. The one exception occurs when complaints against inspectors are received. Not only do these suggest that something has gone wrong that might have been detected earlier, but because of the very nature of complaint investigation, the concerns tend to focus on specific incidents rather than the inspector's whole performance. Inspection by the Audit Commission and the statistical returns to central government have provided another kind of check. These, however, have tended to focus on meeting time scales and adhering to procedures, a legitimate, but narrow focus. As Hopkins says:

> Carrying out the required *number* of inspections may well be a performance indic-
> ator for a unit, but there should be a way of measuring the quality of an
> inspection as well as the quantity. Inspectors could spend 15 minutes in each
> home, meet the target and be praised by the Audit Commission and Social
> Services Inspectorate in a joint review as a well performing unit. Whereas, in
> reality, it is simply a dangerous one. (Hopkins 2000: 31)

This is not to say that failure to meet targets is itself proof that inspections are being conducted with more intensity and professional skill. It does mean that ways have to be found additional to individual supervision and measuring of performance indic-ators to judge the quality of the inspection work being conducted and that providers need to know about and have grounds for confidence in these measures.

All that I have said so far presumes a readiness on both sides to deal sensibly with each other and to demonstrate respect even when differences of opinion may arise. This will be especially important when the first inspections are conducted under the aegis of the Early Years Directorate. We know from the experience of implementing the Children Act that the first inspections of many providers went badly because of the anxieties on both sides. The same heightened anxiety is likely to be there when providers are Early Years Directorate inspected for the first time. At the very least allowance needs to be made for that and every effort should be made to ensure both parties feel as confident as possible in the new situation.

Involving parents in the process of assessment

There is still a great deal to be done to make relationships between providers and childcare inspectors as productive as possible. There is even further to go in relation to parents. It is widely accepted among childcare inspectors, as it is among providers, that cooperation with parents is important, but achievement of this cooperation has been problematic. There are a number of reasons for this.

One is that people are parents of young children for comparatively short periods of their lives now that families tend to be smaller. There are consequent limits to the extent to which people identify themselves with the role of 'parent of young children' (as opposed to other forms of identity to which they can lay claim). Parents may organise at a local level around the need to fill a gap in provision for play, care or education (although that seems to be less common now than it was in the 1960s and 1970s) or they may organise on a wider geographical level around certain issues (as in the case of parents of children with specific medical conditions). Parents as such are unorganised. This is why the local partnerships have had limited success in meeting the requirement that they involve parents in their work. There is a lack of representative bodies with which inspectors can speak. Representative bodies are not always as representative as they claim, but contact with them is an obvious starting point for consultation. Even where representative bodies exist, as in parent groups attached to community nurseries, they are not routinely involved in the process of inspection unless the nursery manager chooses to initiate this. Because such bodies are rare, their consultation does not get into the procedure manuals. This is something that should be corrected by the Early Years Directorate.

A related point is that many parents who use childcare and education services are in full-time employment or engaged in other time-consuming activity. There will be limits to their availability for involvement in assessments and the time they have is least likely to coincide with the time their child is at the provision.

Parents who have concerns may feel nervous about raising them with the provider or the childcare inspector because of the perceived potential repercussions. There is still not enough effective choice for most parents for them to risk offending the provision their children attend without overwhelming reason. It is the common experience of childcare inspectors that the most frequent type of situation in which they are directly approached by parents is the one where a childcare arrangement has broken down and the parent wishes to complain. Such situations may be good indicators of weakness at a provision (weakness in communicating with parents, if not weakness in the area the complaint involves), but there should be other and more positive contributions parents can make to the evaluation of a provision.

Parents may fail to understand the criteria that childcare inspectors are bringing to their evaluations. Suspicion can easily be aroused by references in inspection service documents to child protection or equal opportunities or certain types of play activity if the reasons for attaching importance to these things are not explained.

Finally, it can be noted that the ways that inspection teams have adopted to establish the views of parents are often inadequate. The most common of these is the questionnaire survey conducted around the time of inspection. However well these are designed, they, like all forms, give people limited opportunities to express their views. Childcare inspectors have also been uncertain how to use the results they obtain. Are they to be treated as opinion surveys whose results must be given in inspection reports in tabular form (in spite of their methodological weaknesses by the standards of social scientists)? Is a critical comment made by one person to be highlighted in the report? How far can they be used to give some direction to the observations made at inspection itself?

The task of involving parents in inspections is one fraught with difficulty and no one should be surprised that the performance of childcare inspection teams to date has been poor in relation to this aspect of their work. It does, however, have to be faced that success is limited so far and this is a weakness in the inspection system. It not only detracts from the value of inspection reports, it feeds into the situation throughout the early years field where glib comments about what parents as a species are like have become commonplace. New ways of involving parents have to be found and need the backing of other arrangements. One of the reasons for seeking close connections between local Children's Information Services and local childcare inspection teams is that those services are in contact with parents in situations where their concerns and aspirations may emerge more readily than they do in contact with a regulatory regime.

Involving children in the process of assessment

However limited the achievement, the idea that attempts should be made to involve parents in inspection is common. The idea that children can be directly involved is less usual.

At first this is surprising. One of the issues childcare inspectors are likely to examine is the extent to which children are allowed choice, initiative and creativity in the curriculum offered by a provider. If the provider is expected to treat children this way, why not the inspector?

One reason is that, in spite of support for the principle of involving children in the running of units, there is often uncertainty as to how to go about it. There is also a well-established habit of thought that because young children cannot easily join in the kind of formal discussions that constitute the basis of most citizen participation, they cannot be consulted by public authorities. In a briefing paper issued jointly by the Children's Society and the Community Development Foundation that urges the active involvement of children in community activity, the authors ask whether there can be community development with the under-fives themselves 'or should it focus on families and parents in particular?' (Heaton and Sayer 1992: 14) and most of their examples of successful community development with children involve young adolescents. Fox Harding in her analysis of approaches to childcare policy notes that none of the three basic approaches she identifies entail the idea of children as active participants in their own welfare and thus she adds a 'children's rights' perspective as a fourth approach. She also expresses reservations about talking exclusively in terms of rights as this 'appears to owe more to a cognitive or cerebral approach to other persons than to emotions and spontaneity' which may provide an inadequate understanding of children's needs (Fox Harding 1997: 139). Both her highlighting of the issue of children's rights and her reservations about an excessively legalistic understanding of the subject seem to me as useful in the context of children's day care as they are in the context of child protection which she addresses.

Of course, the behaviour of children and what it suggests about the extent to which children feel themselves cared for and supported in their learning are often subjects for comment in inspection reports. Even that does not happen all the time and is not necessarily emphasised. Reference to direct comment by children in the inspector's notes or the report itself cannot be found as a matter of routine.

In part this is connected with the idea of objectivity resting on detachment. Precisely because it is so easy for a childcare inspector to engage with children, there is sometimes the feeling that this will detract from the business of observation and is something to be avoided. One sometimes hears people speculating on what should be done if the inspector realises that a child is in danger and that this has not yet been noticed by the staff. Should she intervene? How great does the danger have to be before intervention is necessary though a matter for regret? Penn, writing as someone engaged in research in a foreign country rather than as a childcare inspector, shows how strong can be the urge not to engage with children, in the name of objectivity:

> Some of the children were also keen to draw me into their games and were puzzled by my poor vocabulary and pronunciation. I tried to act as neutrally as possible and to avoid eye contact so that children would lose interest in me, but some of the children who approached me were very charming and persistent and it would have been peculiar and clumsy to them if I had continued to ignore them, so then I did smile and show interest in what they offered to me. (Penn 1997: 46)

As a foreigner in a Spanish nursery, Penn was probably more intriguing than the average childcare inspector (childcare inspectors who are men or who are black often have similar experiences). Not everyone will be faced with what she seems to have seen as a dilemma. The fact that children may not be interested in a strange grown-up in the room does not dispose of the matter. I would argue that not only does one have to avoid being clumsy with children who are unlikely to understand the role of the detached observer because they have not yet read the appropriate textbooks or procedure manuals, but that there are positive advantages to engaging with children and seeking to discover something of their experience. They are the people most likely to know whether the provider's self-presentation accords with the daily facts or not.

Of course, it will be difficult to secure children's opinions. As in any opinion gathering, there will be a high risk of subjectivity (the charming child may gain undue influence in constructing the picture of children's views; the awkward child may give a misleading impression because of a degree of unhappiness that stems from outside the provision). However, the ability to understand what people are saying is a key skill in regulation and it is worth asking how adequate an inspector's understanding of children is if she finds that significantly more difficult with children than with adults.

Part of the problem is that it is quite inappropriate to secure children's opinions in the way we often attempt to secure those of grown-ups. There is not much point giving three-year-olds questionnaires to complete. On the other hand, Kinney and McCabe (2001) have practical suggestions on seeking children's opinions by asking them to stick smiling or sad faces onto pictures of activities or different rooms in a unit to secure an initial statement of opinion. They also point out the need to follow up these statements of opinion with discussion as the results can sometimes surprise. Kinney and McCabe were talking about consultation of children by the staff who work with them directly, but the techniques they explain could be used effectively in the context of inspection. To reassure the children (and to help in staff development) it would be preferable if such opinion gathering were done in conjunction with the staff. There is also the consideration that when coaxed out of them young children's views are sometimes expressed with an almost brutal simplicity and the involvement of staff is likely to be needed if the exercise is to be a learning experience for them rather than representing a threat. Another approach, if it can be arranged, is for the inspector to ask to be shown round the unit by a couple of the children and to leave the conduct of the tour entirely to them, without asking questions. This can show up aspects that might not emerge in other ways. The 'shadowing' of particular children, a device developed by people researching early years services, can help the childcare inspector to see the pattern of the nursery's day from the perspective of the child. Mealtimes can be an opportunity to engage children in conversation if the inspector sits with them. Apart from direct engagement it is useful to make efforts to adopt the child's perspective. Drawings and paintings by children who have reached an age when something like realistic representation is within their range can say a great deal. It needs some self-confidence and good humour on the part of both the inspector and inspected, but crawling round on the floor of a childminder's house can show up features of the home that may be important to the child's experience, but are not so obvious to an adult standing up.

We have a long way to go in even considering whether the children who are our focus of concern should also be active participants in the process of assessment. The complexity of the issue is the reason why it should be addressed not a reason why it should be evaded.

Registration, inspection, investigation and enforcement

One of the difficulties OFSTED has faced in taking on the task of regulating early years services is that it is more than inspection that is involved. In their other work they have been concerned almost exclusively with inspection. They have not had to decide that schools were fit to operate before they began doing so. They did have a decision of that kind to make in the initial recognition of eligible providers under the nursery grant scheme, but were aided in those decisions by the fact that all providers that applied had already been registered under the Children Act if they were not schools, so that key decisions were already made.

Regulation as a continuing process can promote the development of providers in a way that inspection alone does not. Whether or not it is the best way of going about things, an inspection system can operate on the basis of snapshots, of sharp observation of the situation at a particular point in time. Regulators are more involved in the life histories of the services they regulate. This may be in a merely negative way – that is to say, the accumulation of evidence over time that a provider is failing and should, perhaps, lose registration status. It can be approached in a more positive spirit. If the objective is to promote quality and not just to detect and deal with failures to meet standards, then it becomes even more important to face up to the consequences of the continuity of contact a regulating agency has with the regulated.

Under the Children Act some childcare inspection teams have approached this issue by means of an organisational division between registration and inspection. Some staff have dealt with initial registrations. Others have been responsible for annual inspections and investigations. Issues arising from either of these (where there are grounds for thinking improvement is possible rather than that de-registration is necessary) are referred back to the registration team who provide direct support or negotiate contact with provider networks, training agencies or others better able to offer sustained support. Those who have used this system like it. However, one of the findings of Candappa *et al.* (1996: 89) was that childcare inspection teams tended to be 'in support of the organisational style and culture in which they currently worked' so their approval has limited relevance. It is also the case that many of these units are quite small and based within single offices so that the registration and the inspection workers were less likely to grow apart and develop different professional cultures. The arrangement adopted in Kirklees offers an example. It cannot be assumed that the advantages some have found in a registration/inspection split would be replicated in the much larger organisation that the Early Years Directorate will be.

Whether or not there are different staff dealing with initial registration, it has to be clear that this must not be a merely administrative exercise, as was possible in the case of eligible providers. OFSTED recognised this and were making clear by the beginning of 2001 that on-the-spot assessment by childcare inspectors would be a key part of the registration process. It is not just that there are issues around the fitness of the premises that involve more than form filling by applicants. (That could be handled in a merely procedural manner with the Early Years Directorate checking on planning permissions and entitlement to use property and commissioning evaluation reports from the fire and rescue service and environmental health officers.) There is a strong developmental element in initial registration assessments. While some applicants for registration will be businesses or voluntary organisations with considerable experience in establishing services in different parts of the country, the majority of group care services and all childminders are small ventures that lack prior experience and may need guidance in developing their plans for the service they wish to offer.

In many cases advice and support will be available from early years development workers in the local authority, the relevant provider network or some other agency. Even then it should be part of the registration service's function to facilitate contact with such people and there will be cases where these services are better established and resourced than they are elsewhere. The 'detached' model of assessment would have the childcare inspector (or someone at the regional office of the Early Years Directorate) examining the application and other evidence that has come in and arriving at a decision. Applicants themselves are likely to find it more helpful if the criteria for registration, the thinking behind those criteria and the reasons why an application is not yet acceptable are clearly explained in a continuing dialogue. In this respect it is important to look critically at the process that is sometimes described as 'counselling out', that is to say, where an applicant is encouraged to withdraw. All too often this has entailed an acceptance that the application is going to be rejected if the applicant persists rather than an understanding of why this should be the case, let alone any coming to terms with the implications for herself of the reasons for potential applications. In such situations the word 'counselling' is being seriously abused. Another issue is that of time scales. At present the Government expects that decisions will be made on applications to register full day-care nurseries within six months and on all other services within three months. Those time scales are often exceeded, not because the childcare inspection team is dilatory but because the applicant has difficulty for one reason or another (such as the vagaries of funding regimes or difficulties in completing construction work to schedule) in attaining the required standard. It would do them no favours simply to reject their applications in order to adhere to time scales. Similarly, if decisions are made without adequate evidence (though in the absence of clear indications against registration) in order to adhere to time scales there is a severe risk that a service will be established on a basis that is not viable and will either fail to attract custom or fall victim to enforcement procedures in a short period of time. It is not in the interests of children or their parents that services be allowed to register that are at risk of failure. I am horrified to learn of the number of newly registered services that collapse within a year or two in some local authorities. It seems to me clear evidence of failure on the part of the childcare inspection team as well as on the part of the providers concerned.

Where a cooperative relationship between the provider and the childcare inspection team is established at the point of registration, the provider will often continue to look to the service for advice. Some childcare inspection teams have made it a matter of routine to contact providers a few weeks or months after initial registration to check on progress. Regular inspection should provide a particular opportunity for providers to review their progress and re-formulate plans for the future as well as providing a means of checking on those that fall significantly below standard.

The positive use of inspection as a resource for self re-evaluation by the provider gives rise to the question of the frequency of inspection. The Care Standards Act leaves to the discretion of the Secretary of State the determination of the normal intervals between inspections. The guidance issued under the 1968 Act spoke of inspections at six-monthly intervals. The Children Act made annual inspections a requirement. A much greater effort was made to conduct inspections under the Children Act, but there was some uncertainty as to how extensive each inspection should be. Coming under pressure to meet performance targets, some local authorities made each inspection less extensive, focusing on the more obvious risks of harm to children rather than the positive qualities of providers and on their curriculum planning and delivery in particular. It is not yet clear how good the resources of the Early Years Directorate will be. However, given the hoped-for expansion under the National Childcare Strategy, there is at least the possibility of tension arising between extensive and frequent inspection. The resolution of that tension must be based on a critical evaluation of the alternatives rather than on a hasty compromise.

If it is possible to see registration and inspection as supportive processes, it is less easy to do the same for investigations with the possibility of de-registration or some other sanction. However, a great deal depends on the spirit in which investigation is conducted or received. While there will be some situations that cannot be tolerated and sanctions will have to be applied, in many cases a provider willing to learn can gain from the consequences of an investigation. It may show up weaknesses the provider can address. Some things are essential if this is to happen. One is that as far as possible parents and other carers are encouraged to raise their own concerns directly with providers and seek resolution of them. Another is that providers are in most cases given the opportunity to conduct their own investigations into allegations made against particular members of staff. A third is that the investigation does not focus exclusively on the facts around a particular incident – facts which are often difficult to ascertain in retrospect – but considers the indications of *possible* problems. Whether something happened may be less important than the fact that the provision operates in such a way that it could have happened. Unfortunately, the danger of legal action often leads both provider and inspector to concentrate on whether the truth of an allegation can be proved in court rather than on the weakness the investigation may have demonstrated. Fourthly, it is important that there are clear policies on enforcement of which all staff in the regulatory service are aware and which have a rational basis. Practice on enforcement has varied from local authority to local authority more than any other aspect of regulation under the Children Act, some resorting to enforcement frequently because they see their function in purely protective terms, others avoiding enforcement except in extreme circumstances because they see regulation linked to support. Even worse, there has often been a see-saw movement between rush to enforcement and timid avoidance of it in response to particular court decisions. This is something that could have been avoided if there had been clearer criteria in operation to determine when enforcement should be initiated. Finally, it is important that, except in cases of abuse or deliberate neglect of safety, it is recognised that weaknesses are the shadow side of strengths, that, for example, inadequate planning for a particular aspect of a provision may be the negative by-product of the energy and desire to achieve quickly that has been the strength of a community enterprise. The acknowledgement of this aspect of any weakness shown is an important part of the overall assessment of an investigation and may make it easier for the provider to accept and act upon the results of that investigation.

The existing childcare inspection teams have varied considerably in the extent to which they have been ready to resort to enforcement notices, interviews under PACE (Police and Criminal Evidence Act) conditions or criminal prosecution. It can be expected that the Early Years Directorate will develop procedures to determine how decisions in this sphere will be taken. It is just as important that a policy is developed which makes clear to its own staff and others how such action is seen within the broad scope of regulation.

The particular case of childminding

Most of what has been said so far in this chapter applies equally to childminders and to group care providers. (The reference to group care as 'day care' in the legislation and the consequent withholding of that title from childminding is an unfortunate use of words that should be reversed.) There are, however, some particular issues relating to childminding that concern determining how far regulation can be a supportive process.

Many of these relate to the history of regulation. Up until the late 1980s there were comparatively few independent nurseries and playcare services for school age children were not covered by the legislation. Work on childcare inspection in the social services departments concentrated to a very considerable extent on childminding and it was often the task of staff specialising in this work to recruit and support childminders to provide a resource for fieldwork colleagues engaged in family support. Those who worked with childminders sometimes also worked in the field of fostering and were influenced by the much more extensive social work literature on support to foster carers in the way they understood their role with childminders. As with fostering, this often meant not merely support to individual minders but also work on the development of local groups for mutual support, organisation and delivery of training, the generation of resources such as 'libraries' for play and safety equipment and the defence of childminders against any tendency to exploitation by colleagues anxious to find quick solutions to some of their clients' problems.

Where this kind of work was undertaken most effectively, childminding as a service area remained under the control of the childcare inspection workers and was a significant source of work satisfaction to them. This was not necessarily a problem in the short term. The arrangements were often seen by childminders themselves as supportive rather than controlling.

The new emphasis on inspection after 1991 did something to undermine all this, but it remained an important part of the work for many childcare inspectors. Unfortunately, it also inhibited the development of childminding as a separate profession. For all the effort that childcare inspectors engaged in it had put into trying to secure a more positive image for childminding, they had probably contributed indirectly to the idea that childminding was a less professional, less trustworthy form of childcare. This was especially the case after 1991 because childcare inspectors were often no longer in a position to put as much time into positive support as they had done in the past.

In my own local authority in Sheffield a number of measures were taken to tackle this problem. Conferences on the future of childminding were organised in 1998 and 1999. A small group of experienced childminders who had trained as trainers were helped by both the childcare inspection team and the capacity-building team in the Young Children's Service to set up a cooperative agency which was able to enter into a service agreement with the childcare inspection team for the delivery of pre-registration courses. As the course was similar in content to the CACHE accredited course on 'Introducing Childminding Practice' it was made possible for those on the course to secure a national qualification. Funding was found through the partnership to appoint a development worker to work with the city-wide Sheffield Childminding Association which was given a new lease of life and secured a better position to deal with others, including the childcare inspection team. Money was also found for the NCMA to appoint one worker initially to attempt to form one or more NCMA accredited network in the city with the consequent possibility that some childminders would secure eligible provider status. There was some regret among the childcare inspection team that a final break was being made with the past relationship with childminders, but it was recognised that some kind of change had already happened which the move to the Early Years Directorate would reinforce and that there had been some enormous gains in the increasing independence and self-reliance of the local childminding service. Similar moves have happened in many other local authorities.

However, it is not just down to accidents of history that childminding has a different relationship to childcare inspectors than that of group care providers and some key factors will remain.

One is that of the different implications of the Protection of Children Act 1999 for childminders and group care providers. That Act places obligations on those that engage people to work with children to run certain checks on them. A fear that some providers will be too ill-informed, careless or dishonest to meet their obligations under that Act has led many childcare inspectors to insist that the Early Years Directorate will still need to run its own checks. It is true that particular effort would need to be put into ensuring that providers were conforming to POCA regulations, but it is difficult to see how the duplication of checks could be justified. The case of childminders is different. They cannot be expected to check their own households and act upon the information received. The Early Years Directorate will continue to be responsible for checks on them and this may be felt to have some significance.

Of more fundamental importance is the fact that childminders operate by and large on their own. Many can rely on the support of their own families. Some have registered assistants or approved joint childminding arrangements. Some belong to relatively informal local groupings of childminders and an increasing number may be expected to join NCMA accredited networks. Nevertheless, they spend most of their working time on their own or at best working alongside one other person. They are, therefore, more likely to look to childcare inspectors for support and advice for at least some time to come.

There are also practical aspects of the conduct of inspections. The checking of record systems and of continuing safety in the home and the discussion of issues often have to take place when the minded children are present. This is quite different from the situation in group care inspections. It becomes particularly acute if the minder wishes to discuss concerns about a particular child when one of the children is present, though that can often be deferred for a later visit or telephone call to the office. (One of the questions about home-based working in the Early Years Directorate is how that sort of discussion will be managed.) It is also difficult to observe childminders interacting with children in the way that it is possible to observe staff in a group care setting. The fact that the number of people present is much smaller and that they are more likely to be physically close to each other makes the detached form of observation more or less impossible and creates particular difficulties for other types of observation. Thus inspections of childminders often become social work interviews at some cost to the child who is supposed to be receiving care and attention. The question of the self-confidence of the provider becomes crucial here. Childminders do not always appreciate that they are likely to go up rather than down in the estimation of the childcare inspector if they give priority to the care of the children at the expense of discussion with her.

Finally, there is the fact that the childminder's home is precisely her home and not just a place of work. There is something potentially intrusive about conducting assessments in the minder's home and especially about the conduct of home safety checks. The garden may be a place for quiet and relaxation for the family that owns it, but is likely to hold more potential hazards than the home itself in the eyes of the inspector. To be at once a workplace inspector and a guest in someone's home requires considerable tact. Childcare inspectors with backgrounds in social work have often found the dilemmas easier to tackle than those who have previously operated in group care settings.

There is a particular history to the relationship between childminders and childcare inspectors that goes some way to explaining why the task of assessing them feels different. But more than the history is involved and many of the dilemmas will remain if (or when) childminding is better established as a professional service with its own support mechanisms.

Accreditation and quality assurance

This chapter has challenged the idea that regulation, on the one hand, and support and development, on the other, are two discrete areas of work which can and should be totally separate. It has been suggested that regulation can for much of the time have a supportive aspect. In a book on support and development I might have talked about the other side of the coin, about the obligations of development workers not to collude with poor practice, not just in the interests of children, but to protect the interests of providers whose success and self-esteem must rest in the end on the quality of the service they provide.

However, the issue is not just about how the two activities relate to each other. There is also another form of activity which has a separate existence and appears to fall somewhere in between the two. The last decade has seen the development of a large number of quality assurance or accreditation systems in the childcare field and it is necessary to look at how these influence the picture. This has become particularly important now that the Government has said it wishes to see 40 per cent of providers achieving accreditation by quality assurance regimes by 2004.

It is time that there was a survey of the accreditation and quality assurance schemes that are now available and that some attempt was made to judge their effectiveness. There is no quality assurance scheme for quality assurance schemes. The DfEE has constructed a list of such schemes, but was at pains initially to say that inclusion on the list is not an indication of official approval. This was a little naive. It is inevitable that providers will see inclusion on the list as evidence of approval. Indeed, what would the DfEE do about its list if it became clear that a particular scheme was seriously defective? In fact, by the end of 2000 the DfEE had already arrived at criteria for inclusion of schemes on their list.

One of the difficulties in assessing the existing schemes is that the variety is considerable. To take just some of the major sources of variety:

- Some schemes, such as the Sheffield Kitemark, are organised for all types of providers on a local level while others operate nationally and are designed to meet the needs of particular types of provider (NDNA, NCMA, PLA and Kids' Clubs Network all have schemes of this latter type).
- Some operate on the basis of what is, in effect, an inspection to judge the provider against the criteria adopted by the scheme, while others operate on an incremental model with providers able to secure units of the accreditation over a period of time.
- Some have a significant measure of self-assessment, while others rely entirely on the observations of outside assessors.
- Some focus exclusively on the quality of direct work with children, while others also take into account questions of business efficiency and the ways in which the provider is making the service viable (even if it operates on a not-for-profit basis).

Those involved in such schemes sometimes suggest that they are a more effective way of promoting quality than the regulatory regime.

To some extent this may be based on experience in particular areas that suggests a restricted role for regulation. Certainly, the impression is given that in some areas the childcare inspection teams were not involved in the construction of some of the locally based quality assurance regimes beyond giving their approval on the basis that nothing that was said contradicted local requirements of registered providers. In other areas childcare inspection teams have played a significant role in the development of local accreditation schemes.

In some cases it is clear that an ideological point is being made. Even where the local childcare inspection regime has had a wider scope (has, for example, taken on board curriculum issues), the quality assurance regime is felt to be better because it does not have the force of law and has a strong voluntary element.

However, as accreditation regimes take hold they cannot remain in any absolute sense voluntary. The scheme for the accreditation of playcare activities that receive only children over eight (and are not, therefore, subject to registration) is closely linked to the Working Families Tax Credit and it will become financially unwise for many providers to avoid seeking that accreditation. The authors of the DfEE report *Tomorrow's Children* accepted that less formal groups such as parent and toddler groups should not be subject to registration but did suggest 'the development of voluntary quality assurance arrangements covering these groups, particularly in areas such as premises and health and safety' (DfEE 1999, para. 147), clearly seeing quality assurance as some kind of substitute for regulation. It is also significant that the word 'monitoring' creeps into descriptions of some local quality assurance regimes. Although local authorities with provision for a majority of four-year-olds in mainstream schools have developed quality assurance systems as a way of driving up standards and encouraging dialogue between different types of providers, many of those who have developed such systems have most of their educational provision for three- and four-year-olds offered by registered services that are eligible providers under the nursery grant scheme. There have been concerns in some of those authorities that they would have difficulty in ensuring that the services purchased by the LEAs were good enough and quality assurance regimes have been developed as a way of offering some kind of guarantee. It is in such authorities that terms such as 'monitoring' begin to appear in descriptions of the systems available and there is clearly some element of contract compliance, even if it is neither well thought out nor explicit.

Another advantage claimed for quality assurance systems over regulatory ones is that they allow for self-assessment. Again, this comparison is too simple. Not all accreditation systems give any priority to self-assessment, while those childcare inspection teams that have worked on a more supportive, less detached model have tried to build elements of self-evaluation into the registration and inspection processes.

Quality assurance and accreditation systems are in part a product of the fragmentation of the early years scene. They are responses to local issues or to issues affecting particular types of provider. It remains to be seen how they will develop once a national system of regulation is well established. As has been argued above, the distinction between quality assurance and inspection can be too firmly drawn. Certainly the range of issues covered in most quality assurance frameworks and most local registration guidelines are remarkably similar. Where there are differences this is often a reflection of growing sensitivity in the most innovative parts of the early years sector to some aspects of provision where opportunities for enhancing quality are apparent but some childcare inspection regimes are still exclusively focused on health and safety (the curriculum aspects of outdoor play and children's meals would be obvious examples). The inspection regime might be expected to catch up with current thinking, even if it does not do so quickly enough.

All this is not to argue that quality assurance regimes are not needed. They play an important part already and just one of their advantages is that participation in their design has helped some childcare inspection teams to review their perspectives on key issues. What I cannot see happening is a tripartite system of development, quality assurance and regulation with clear demarcation lines between all of them.

Functions retained by local authorities after the transfer

Schedule 2 para. 1 (2) of the Children Act gave local authorities authorisation to publish information about the range of childcare services in their areas and to 'take such steps as are reasonably practicable to ensure that those who might benefit from the services receive the information relevant to them'. There was nothing explicit in the Act about support, including funding and training that might be offered to the independent sector. Sections 4.11–17 and chapter 5 of volume 2 of the Guidance and Regulations issued by the Department of Health, which dealt with these issues, were fine so far as they went, but that was not very far. The Care Standards Act changes the situation considerably with new obligations for local authorities created in section 79V. The Act also speaks of regulations on the implementation of the section. Work on those regulations began at the end of 2000 and is due to be completed in the spring of 2001.

Childcare inspection teams had often engaged in such operations under the Children Act, though the scope and nature of that engagement varied widely across the country. Because the Care Standards Act makes clear that it is local authorities and not Her Majesty's Chief Inspector that will have responsibility for such functions, they are referred to as the duties retained by or remaining with the local authorities. Sometimes the term 'residual' has been used. This is an unfortunate phrase since it suggests something small and insignificant in scale. That is not the case. Some local authorities have already invested in this work, though often dependent on external rather than mainstream funding for it and often delivering services on the basis of agreements with partners in the independent sector rather than by the use of their own staff. A few of the larger authorities have been spending very significant sums of money in this area. Even if local authorities are not already investing heavily, the new statutory obligations in section 79V and the requirements in the Guidance for the revised Early Years Plans for the period 2001–4 suggest that they will need to do so. In particular the question arises of whether a greater amount of the mainstream budget should be spent on matters such as information services, training initiatives, the employment (by the authority or by partners) of development workers, capacity builders and mentors and the development of local quality assurance schemes so that there is less dependence on European or other external funding. Changes in the Standard Spending Assessments have made money available to local authorities for this, but there may have to be some hard local negotiations before it happens in practice.

The question of how local authorities should meet their obligations under section 79V or early years partnerships under the Guidance for 2001–4 is outside the scope of this book. There are, however, a number of issues concerning the role of childcare inspection teams in local strategies.

The first is that the disappearance of existing childcare inspection teams will leave some gaps that may not be noticed unless those teams play a part in drafting the local strategy before they disappear. There are two that are obvious. Most childcare inspection teams have run day duty services which have been used as an easily accessible source of help and advice by both parents and providers in a way that will not easily be replicated. The second is that some types of provider do not have national or local networks of their own to which they can look for support, especially in dealing with issues directly relating to regulation. The two most obvious examples are crèches attached to organised adult activities and schemes for 'wrap around' day care set up in close partnership with maintained schools. Even if other types of provider have access to paid development staff employed by provider networks such as PLA, NDNA, NCMA or others, these kinds of providers will not and special provision will have to be made for them if many of the schemes now being launched are to avoid running into serious difficulty.

There is also the issue of how help can be made available to registered services that are of poor quality, but where the goodwill of the providers and the nature of the deficiencies being encountered make sanctions seem a heavy-handed response. Already many local authorities have set up particular mechanisms to ensure that there is supportive intervention in those situations where eligible providers have had a number of critical nursery grant inspections. The extension of the scope of such bodies to cover all providers or at least all group care services is an obvious step to take. Childcare inspectors have been important to the success of such bodies in many of the areas where they exist and the new teams established as part of the Early Years Directorate should look to have such a role in every partnership area.

Finally, there is the question of the way in which assessments conducted by childcare inspectors (registration assessments, inspections and investigations) can help to show up development needs not just of individual providers but across partnership areas. To some extent this will be possible if inspection reports in particular are framed in such a way that it is easy to read off trends and ideas from a number of them and enter them on databases devised to support this kind of work. However, this needs to be supplemented by the participation of inspectors in sub-groups of the early years childcare & development partnerships that are particularly concerned with matters of quality and training. This will be one of the key roles of the senior childcare inspectors in particular.

Conclusion

The central issue addressed in this chapter has been the extent to which regulatory assessments should be conducted in a detached or in a more supportive manner.

I believe that it is important that regulation is undertaken in a supportive manner and – to the extent that the responsibilities allow – in partnership with providers. It is not easy to do this, but unless it is done there will always be the risk that providers will not take full responsibility for their actions or for the overall promotion of quality in the services they offer. It is too easy for a provider to hide behind the apparent approval of the regulatory service and evade responsibility. This is in spite of the fact that approval in this situation is often a hesitation to disapprove to the point of enforcement. Policing is necessary because of the constant possibility that something will go wrong. But policing itself depends for its success on the support of the policed. A state that had to have a policeman on every corner every moment of the day would soon collapse. A regulatory service that tries to ensure it has checked everything that is going on is doomed to fail and may well miss some important problems while busily scampering through an almost endless check list.

I not only believe it is important, I am optimistic that it can be done. This is not the same as being optimistic that it will be done. My optimism rests on the fact that nearly all those involved – childcare inspectors, providers, their staff, development workers, planners and trainers – have a real interest in the welfare of children. They give more than notional consent to the idea. In my experience there is a real and widespread commitment. That commitment of the many should not prevent us from being alert to the small number who do not share it nor to the fact that even those who are best intentioned may get things seriously wrong. But neither should we spend so much time looking at the things that might go wrong that we miss the opportunities that the commitment of people and some aspects of the current politics of childcare offer. It is the shared commitment that makes possible real partnership between all those involved in the local early years plans, including the childcare inspectors. We just need to work at it and have confidence in what we are trying to do.

Chapter 5

Getting serious: aspects of quality

Introduction

The scope of regulation was discussed in the last chapter in terms of general principle. This chapter looks at that issue in terms of four of the factors that might be considered in making an assessment of an early years provision:

- health and safety;
- equal opportunities;
- outdoor play;
- music.

It should go without saying that these have not been selected because they are the most important for a childcare inspector to consider. It is because the first two could be said to have been taken too seriously and the latter two not seriously enough. As a result consideration of them helps us to examine the relationship in inspection work between action to prevent harm and action to promote quality.

The word 'seriously' is being used here in two different senses. It is an indicative idiosyncrasy of the English language that it does not distinguish as readily as some others between what is serious in the sense of being a source of worry and what is serious in the sense of being important. Health and safety and equal opportunities have been treated with too much gravity, seen simply as occasions for things to go wrong unless vigilance prevents it. Outdoor play and music, on the other hand, are not always ascribed as much importance as should be the case. Both defects follow from a restricted understanding of regulation. That approach keeps childcare inspection – and to some extent, therefore, provision – within the boundaries of what is to be avoided rather than keeping them open to opportunity. That is in the end a way of undermining standards.

Health and safety

The reader may have read William Goldman's novel *Marathon Man* or seen the film version with Dustin Hoffman and Laurence Olivier. The fairly complex plot can be summarised as follows: a Nazi is forced to leave his Latin-American hiding place to come to New York to fetch a collection of diamonds that will keep him in relative comfort for the rest of his life. He is terrified of discovery and goes to extraordinary and violent lengths to reassure himself of his security before going to the bank where the diamonds rest in a deposit box. 'Is it safe?' he asks constantly. In the end his frantic efforts to ensure his safety precipitate the events that lead to his death.

Something like that has happened in early years services in this country. Asking constantly 'Is it safe?' we have inhibited ideas on how services can be developed and may have created new problems along the way.

This has certainly been the view of some critics from outside the regulation system. The Jacksons in their study of childminding were critical of the limited understanding of children's welfare that went into the operation of the 1948 Act (Jackson and Jackson 1979). Penn, contrasting attitudes in the UK and in Spain, as revealed in her research, writes:

> Whereas the Spanish nurseries had been relaxed about health and safety and administrators considered even unsafe premises could be used by competent staff, the UK nurseries were by contrast almost hysterical about safety … The Children Act which regulates daycare provision has a substantial section on health and safety regulations which has been zealously interpreted by those responsible for registration and inspection, because they are perceived as tangible and incontrovertible evidence of caring. If every conceivable risk is identified and removed, then parents can be assured of their children's safety and registration officers can be seen to have done their duty. But such anaesthetized, unventilated, surveyed spaces are dreary and constricting for the children themselves. They offer no opportunities for fun, games, co-operation, secrecy, exploration, movement, exertion or challenge or even fresh air. (Penn 1997: 89 and 131–2)

This comment is sweeping and has at least a touch of hyperbole. Things may have been as bad as that in the situations she and the Jacksons examined. The picture is not one that is universally accurate. Nevertheless, there is a strong element of truth in it. When childcare inspectors react angrily to jibes from some educationists that 'they only count the toilets' they demonstrate by their very sensitivity that they recognise some justification in the accusation.

The sting lies in Penn's phrase 'If every conceivable risk is identified and removed', since that often seems to be the objective. The trouble is that, like the Nazi in Goldman's novel, we are then up against the dilemma that too much effort in a given direction produces the opposite effect to that intended. It would be possible to create an environment in which 'every conceivable risk' that the child would come to accidental harm was eliminated, but in all probability the child's muscles would atrophy and she would go mad. Being alive is a risky business and if we want children to live (in every sense of that word), we must not try to eliminate risk, but to assess it carefully and act upon those assessments. This is rendered difficult by a number of factors.

There is first of all the history. Regulation of early years services began with moral panics over accidental deaths in the homes of childminders. The real and powerful source of those panics was probably a patriarchal desire to get women back to the kitchen sink, but those who stirred up panic focused on the quite irrefutable assertion that no one would want a child to die as the result of an accident. Hence regulation was first sited in the old public health departments and regulation was focused from the first on safety.

Another factor is that this focus is a comparatively easy one to adopt. The components of quality in early years services do not lend themselves to mathematical measurement. The two that *appear* to do so are staffing and safety. Staffing does so because it is possible to check the number of staff in relation to the number of children and check how many of them have relevant formal qualifications or criminal records. That kind of measurement is not always helpful. A provision that has half of its staff appropriately qualified and the other half made up of local people with extensive practical experience of caring for children might well provide a better service than one where all staff were recently qualified but all of them lacked experience, especially experience under the direction of more competent colleagues. The fact that it appears to be easy to determine that there is adherence to standards does not always mean that an effective and realistic judgement is being made.

The same is even more true of safety. The inspector can, indeed, count the toilets, measure the height of the fence, check the temperature in the fridge and make a number of other measurements that indicate beyond argument that a specific standard has or has not been met. This is very comforting. It is certainly easier than determining how a nursery is likely to react to signs that could just possibly indicate a case of child abuse. It is this ease and comfort that makes the focus on measurement in health and safety so dangerous.

One reason for this is that even in health and safety what can be measured is not the beginning and end of the story. Too often the question appears to be what could possibly happen to an object the size and texture of a small child. The real question is what anyone would want to do with it, including, crucially, the small child herself.

Safe practice is at least as important as the intrinsic safety of objects. When I hear concerns about staircases in the homes of childminders the first question that occurs to me is why it is imagined the minder will leave a child playing on the stairs at all. Of course, there is the possibility that a staircase will be truly dangerous, but the real issue in most cases is whether the limited risks attached to a drop in level are managed properly by the adult. What is true of the overall design of the premises is true of a whole range of issues, such as food safety and prevention of infections.

It is not only the practice of the adult carer that is at issue. There is also the practice of the child. Young children are conscious of danger and take steps to avoid it. A wariness of steep drops is established well before the first birthday and thus before the child enters the first stages of mobility. However, children need some protection from hazards by their adult carers because there are limits to their cognitive capacities. It is not until about the 16th birthday that the average human being achieves completely competent use of eyesight in the sense of being able to scan everything within vision and respond to stimuli even when they are outside the main focus, seeing things 'out of the corner of your eye' as it is often put. The limited, but constantly developing, ability of children to scan is a primary explanation for the many falls on the level toddlers experience as they learn to walk or, more importantly, the high rate of deaths and serious injuries among child pedestrians who are expected by many drivers to have the same skills as adults in this respect or else to keep off the roads altogether. Similarly, children only gradually develop the ability to put things in narrative sequence. This means that a child that is quite aware that some kind of danger is posed by fire may be unable to construct the hypothetical narrative 'If I twirl round, my nightie will flare out and then it might get near the fire and then it might catch fire and then I might be burned' even though she is capable of understanding any one of the connections between events in the sequence. Thus steps need to be taken to protect children from those forms of harm that follow from their limited abilities. However, we need to focus on their abilities as well as on the limits to those abilities. Children need to be helped to learn how to protect themselves. At first this may entail rote learning of sequences of behaviour whose justification they do not entirely understand. The Green Cross Code and the practice of washing hands at certain points of the day are obvious examples.

Doing that may mean allowing the child to learn for herself. A friend of mine who pioneered work with playschemes in Sheffield in the early 1970s has a piece of film showing a young child trying to decide whether or not to leap from a height in an outside playspace. It is sometimes used in training. If we have plenty of time and are feeling a little cruel we let the film run for its full natural time. Although the child exists only on film (and must by now be a middle-aged woman) it is almost excruciatingly painful to watch her trying to make up her mind whether or not to jump. She is clearly at risk of falling and hurting herself. Surely somebody should intervene before something happens? Nobody does. The child spends several minutes calculating whether she is or is not capable of making the jump, arrives on her own initiative at the correct conclusion and leaps successfully. She then triumphantly repeats the process two or three times in quick succession before skipping away to do something else. The grown-ups that were running that playcare scheme protected her by allowing her both to protect herself (nobody forced her to jump before she was ready) and to take the risk once she had calculated both the risk itself and her own ability to cope. She had thus built up resources for her own self-protection in future as well as enjoying her triumph without any harm.

Trying too hard to protect children can have precisely the opposite effect. At one time it was the practice to box in the tops of slides to prevent children falling out sideways before they had the chance to go down the slide itself. This type of design gave children no opportunity to change their minds about whether they felt confident about tackling the slide. Being jostled by those behind them who wanted their go, they sometimes climbed on to the outside of the box to escape and fell with resulting injuries. More recently installed slides in children's playgrounds are likely to be built into banks to allow for ease of escape from the top of the slide. They can look more dangerous, but are, in fact, safer because they take into account not just the damage that could come from a fall, but the situation that could precipitate a fall. They treat the children as human beings able to make choices rather than objects to be protected.

The attempt to assess risk by measuring against fixed standards is bound in the end to become arbitrary. One has only to think of what happened when the old standards which had been constructed in terms of imperial measurement were translated in the 1990s into metric measurements, so that 25 square feet became 2.3 square metres. This should have made it clear that the original figures could only be an approximate guide to what was reasonable, but by that time the space standards and other measurements had become a matter of faith, never to be questioned.

The potential failure to make proper risk assessment is one reason why focus on the measurable is dangerous. The other is that focus on such things fails to place safety issues in a wider context. Nappy changing is one area where there is often failure in this respect. That nappies should be changed in an efficient manner with close attention to hygiene is essential, but if the search for efficiency and hygiene leads to a production-line operation, the process can be experienced by the child as cold, brutal and invasive rather than caring. The experience of the child is crucial as well as the avoidance of physical harm. All babies are intelligent enough to know this better than some early years professionals. This is one area where inspection itself can cause problems. Nappy changing often takes place in areas specially designated for the purpose. Since they have a restricted function they are usually small. Hence the childcare inspector is often much closer to the member of staff than would normally be the case. This in turn can heighten awareness of being inspected and lead to a more exclusive focus on proper hygiene and an inhibition of any showing of affection or concern.

A second area that could be mentioned is meal times. Penn's anger at the differences she saw between nurseries in this country and abroad is once again apparent:

> In the UK nurseries, mealtimes could be described as grim and dutiful fuelling.
> (Penn 1997: 33)

Goldschmied and Jackson in a more positive vein have a whole chapter on meals seen as opportunities for celebration and interaction (1994: 149–60). On the other hand, a recent book on nursery management has nothing on meals beyond a brief reference to the implications of the Food Hygiene Regulations Act 1990 (Lyus 1998: 193).

Mealtimes are a notoriously difficult aspect of any full day-care setting. The fact that in some respects they represent the part of the day that comes nearest to daily life at home makes the attempt to organise them within an institutional setting problematic.

The fact that family meals are becoming less common with different members of the family having to conform to different daily routines in other respects does not help. The tight financial restraints on many group care settings also render it difficult to supply sufficient staff to allow some to focus on meals and all staff to have adequate breaks.

Yet it is difficult to avoid the suspicion that the real issue is one of attitudes rather than practicality. Penn's description of mealtimes in nurseries in Spain and Italy shows what can be done if meals are seen as important in their own right (Penn 1997). One of the factors influencing this may be the low expectations people have of eating in institutional settings, encouraged by lingering historical memories of meals in the conscripted armed services, in schools, in badly organised works canteens and a whole range of other settings in Britain before the foodie revolution shifted expectations in the 1980s.

A third area is that of premises in general. They can be essentially safe, but just as essentially dull. Official documents laying down standards for premises in other European countries place much more emphasis than most comparable documents from the UK on the attractiveness of the physical environment, factors such as natural light and the ways in which it facilitates learning. Even before responsibility for pre-school services was transferred from the social services to the education sphere in Spain, an official publication on cradle schools (for children aged nought to three years) in Barcelona spoke of the importance of the use of space in a nursery to help children make sense of their world rather than the amount of space available or similar standards (Escayola and Odena 1987).

In speaking of the need for risk assessment as well as the application of precise standards and for issues relating to safety to be put more firmly in the context of the general care of the child, I am not suggesting in any way that safety standards should be relaxed. What I would like is to see them given a new foundation. This is not easy to do. When there were proposals in the Consultation Pack on the new National Standards that some existing measurements be adjusted there was near universal outrage. It was widely felt that any adjustment would mean sacrificing standards to the viability of providers (the way the Consultation Pack presented these proposals did something to confirm such suspicions). But there is nothing wrong with reconsideration. While research and practical experience often suggest that safety standards need to be tightened, they also suggest in many cases that they can be relaxed. Medical advances have made cross-infection between babies in group care settings a much less significant risk than it was a quarter of a century ago. Views on the best materials to use for food chopping boards have changed. Every specific standard needs to be kept under review. While standards retain iconic status there is the risk that they will simply be ignored by some providers (except when preparing for inspection). If the rationale behind them is better understood and they are put in a wider context of concern for the child there is more likelihood that they will be respected and deserve respect.

The reluctance to take such steps has made safety too serious a matter and suggested a conflict between safety and fun. That is a dangerous lesson to be teaching in itself.

Equal opportunities

The case of equal opportunities is in several respects even worse. It is treated by both the inspectors and the inspected as a difficult and problematic area. The team from the Thomas Coram Foundation that were looking at the childcare inspection services established under the Children Act found that:

> In general equal opportunities was considered to be one of the more intangible, qualitative issues within regulation. (Bull *et al.* 1994: 61)

If the issues were seen more in the context of the everyday and of fun, and not in terms of the exotic and excessively serious, there might be fewer difficulties and it might seem less intangible.

In this section, after describing briefly the scope and limits of what the Children Act itself has to say on this topic, I shall argue that the issue has been taken 'seriously' in the wrong sense of the word – made a matter of moralistic judgement and problematic expertise – and then begin to sketch out some of the ways in which childcare inspectors might approach the issue.

Some claim that the commitment to equality of opportunity by childcare inspectors comes from the Children Act. Reference is made to the phrase used in several passages requiring due attention to be paid to the 'religious persuasion, racial origin and cultural and linguistic background' of any child whose needs are being considered in relation to that part of the Act.

This is at best an oversimplification. The phrase makes reference to race and culture rather than any other aspect of equality of opportunity. It is used exclusively in the context of meeting the needs of a specific child receiving a service of some kind and has nothing directly to say about a broader commitment to equal opportunities. (This limited perspective was also reflected in the draft National Day Care Standards which had significantly more to say about protecting individual children from discrimination than they did on the need for an equal opportunities curriculum.) The requirement in the Children Act can also be seen as the natural product of previous legislation and guidance which had sought to offer reassurance to minorities (Catholics and Jews in particular) that childcare and educational initiatives would not be used as recruitment devices by the Church of England.

The fact that childcare inspection teams were, at least initially, set up in social services departments had some impact on the way in which equality of opportunities was seen. In both education and social work such commitment was widespread and upheld by various representative bodies. Indeed, the commitment of both of those professions was a reflection of significant change in relation to women and to a lesser extent black people and an even lesser extent people with disabilities that had occurred in British society over the last half of the 20th century. But there were some differences.

In education, especially in school teaching, there was something of a natural progression from ideas of integration to a more considered approach to the needs of children from minorities and on to concepts of multicultural education and the place of anti-racism, with the Swann Report in 1985 providing a particular focal point. The natural progression connected with the fact that education had always had to deal with children that were different in the context of a universal service. This is not, of course, to say that everything was fine in the world of education. The natural progression was too slow and remains so today. However, there was a contrast with the way that equality of opportunities was taken up in the social services world.

In the course of the 1980s the social work profession saw the undermining of much of the value base that it had developed for itself in the 1950s. The central concept had been the American-imported notion of non-judgementalism. By the 1980s many applications of that idea which had seemed revolutionary in the conformist early 1950s had been adopted by the wider public. It could no longer be seen as specific to the profession. At the same time the increased commitment to protecting children (and to a lesser extent vulnerable adults) from abuse by their carers made much more problematic the idea that 'The special function of social work, and its inalienable element, is to ... promote the interests of the individual client' (British Association of Social Workers 1973, para. 11). In the context of child protection it was no longer obvious who the client was or how far the social worker could be supportive of failing parents. The undermining of the value base made equality of opportunities welcome as offering a new ethical foundation. And in some respects the profession moved from a commitment to non-judgementalism to a highly judgemental attitude focused on this issue.

It was key to all this that the commitment to equal opportunities was seen in moralistic terms. It was forgotten that, however bad it might be in its effects, discrimination has its origins in perfectly sound responses. Those sources are the impulse to generalise and the related impulse to be cautious in situations that are strange. There is nothing essentially wrong with either. If we did not generalise, we would not be able to make sense of the situations in which we find ourselves. If we were not cautious of the unfamiliar, we might run into danger. The difficulty comes when both impulses are allowed to override all others, when generalisation becomes stereotyping or caution becomes fear. Even positive stereotypes are dangerous. To suggest that Afro-Caribbean people have natural rhythm and are good at sport may sound like a positive thing to say. It is unlikely to be helpful to a young black wheelchair user with ambitions to become a nuclear scientist. We have, therefore, to avoid stereotyping, but at the same time we do not need to apologise or feel guilty for the impulse towards generalisation that lies behind it. And yet discrimination and especially racism are often seen in moralistic terms. This comes out especially in responses to discrimination among children.

When it was discovered that children as young as three were showing signs of recognising different skin colours and assigning differential value to them there was widespread horror (Aboud 1988). The horror was based partly on a view of children as innocent. If they have adopted racist ideas their minds must have been corrupted. In educational terms this goes back to the views of the philosopher John Locke who saw children as immigrants newly arrived in this world who had to have the place where they found themselves explained clearly.

Less attention has been paid to the even more interesting research finding that children are at their most prejudiced at the age of four and develop greater tolerance and understanding, especially in relation to third-world countries, as they grow older (Scoffham 1999). There are exceptions to this. For example, primary school children often engage in 'name calling' as a way of handling conflict. Name calling tends to focus on physical features, such as weight or the wearing of spectacles. It can, therefore, involve reference to skin colour or other 'racial' features. Such behaviour is often hurtful – it is meant to be – and it is not to be taken lightly as it can contribute to a black child's experience of racism, but it is not straightforwardly a reflection of an acquired racist ideology. Troyner and Hatcher (1992) clarify this aspect of children's behaviour while highlighting the possible consequences. However, in general it is true that stereotyping is at its strongest when children are in their pre-school years. This form of stereotyping is clearly linked to the child's discovery of the minds of other people, a topic on which there is an increasing amount of research demonstrating the crucial nature of what happens in the third and fourth year (Astington 1994). If the child does not see all minds as like her own, she will not be able fully to appreciate that they have their own perspectives. Hence initial stereotyping is a part of the progress to universal sympathy if the child's development in that direction is properly nurtured. There is a related research finding in the world of disability. Even children who grow up in families where someone (a parent or sibling) has a sensory impairment find it difficult to appreciate the physical consequences until close to their fifth birthday (Lewis 1995: 68).

Of course, the fact that children are particularly liable to stereotypical thinking in the later pre-school years does not mean that there is no problem. They will not just grow out of it. They need help precisely because the urge to seek certainty and order at that stage leaves them vulnerable to ideas that provide false certainty. They must be offered a wider view of the world and of humanity in a whole variety of ways across the curriculum and must be helped sensitively when they get things wrong.

It is not just in relation to race or gender or disability that young children tend to stereotype. It is a prevalent characteristic. A very familiar example is the pre-school child with well-developed language skills who over-regularises the language and says, for example, 'I runned to the house'. A young child who makes that kind of error is likely to arouse quiet amusement and stands a reasonable chance of being corrected gently ('Yes you *ran* quite quickly didn't you?'). A child that makes a similar error and comes out with a prejudiced remark about another child is likely to get a much less satisfactory response, one that is likely to derive from a mixture of shock ('How can an innocent little child say such things?'), guilt ('I sometimes feel that way myself') and uncertainty over a conflict of values ('Can I contradict a belief that obviously comes from the child's parents?'). Whatever the source of the confusion it does not help. Nor does it help simply to tell the child she is wrong. The strength of feeling that lies behind the slide into confusion or the urge to suppress the unwelcome comment from the child also lead too often to a failure to consider the feelings of the child against whom the remark was made and respond to those appropriately. A refusal of guilt is necessary before effective communication with the children is possible. To dispense with a sense of shock and outrage is not to abandon any ethical approach to the issue, but to offer it a more certain foundation.

A tendency to moralise is one source of difficulty in the promotion of equality of opportunity. Much of the difficulty also arises from the notion that the topic deals with the unusual and the exotic. However, if the staff at a childcare service have difficulty responding to a child that is quite evidently different in some way, how will they manage to respond to less obvious differences? If they do not engage properly with children whose language at home is not English, how well are they engaging with other children whose English may deviate from the standard in minor ways? There may be issues of accent. It is common for families to generate a few words of what might be called their own 'dialects' often based on mispro-nunciations or strikingly original phrases their children have used while still at early stages of language development. Staff that are baffled by a completely different language are likely to be insensitive to the potential communication problems when the language of English-speaking children has such minor departures from stand-ard English.

In this respect it is worth remembering that many of the pioneers of thinking about early years services developed their ideas while dealing with children with disabilities, using those particular experiences as the basis for theoretical approaches to work with all children. Montessori and Steiner are among the leading examples.

Their own goodwill often leads staff to imagine there is no problem. In one research project where video and other records demonstrated that staff in multiethnic nurseries treated children differently on the basis of race 'the findings of this research came as a surprise to the staff concerned' (Siraj-Blatchford 1994: 44). Part of the diffi-culty is that some of the currently popular theoretical approaches to children's learning do not take equal opportunities fully into account. (Again the issue of interconnect-edness is key.) Gregory suggests that:

> Although both Vygotsky and Bruner's work may be interpreted on a socio-cultural plane with far more complex implications. It has been more manageable for classroom practitioners to concentrate on the one-to-one interaction between teacher and child. As a consequence, Bruner's notion of a 'joint culture creation' between pupil and teacher has often been seen as unproblematic as long as teachers have a firm grounding in general theories of child language and devel-opment. (Gregory 1997: 3)

In other words, educational theory can, if misapplied, lead into a more sophisticated version of 'I treat them all the same'. This becomes especially crucial in the case of those children whose home language is other than English, the issue with which Gregory is primarily concerned.

Recognition of difference makes the achievement of real equality easier. Lewis cites the research evidence demonstrating that if contact is established between children with special educational needs and others in a context in which the difference is clearly acknowledged, this appears to work more effectively than if there is no clear categorisation and comments that 'This is a fascinating finding and one which, at first, seems to run counter to intuition' (Lewis 1995: 58).

Recognition of difference can be a challenge to seek connection and understanding. I recently spent some time with a small group of seven- and eight-year-old white children looking at an Indian comic. The comic showed in strip cartoon form a story from Mahabharata. One of the children was puzzled because the characters in the story looked to him Asian, but the writing was not, i.e. it was in the Hindi Devanagari script rather than the Urdu Nastaliq script that could be seen in local Asian shops. This led to a brief discussion about different calligraphies. The idea was extremely strange to some of them. Thus difference was highlighted. At that stage the discussion could have ended on a note of mild curiosity at best or, at worst, hostility to people that are different. What prevented this was that the children recognised with ease the strip cartoon form and responded to it. Somewhat to my surprise, they went to some effort over a period of a few minutes to attempt to reconstruct the story from the pictures alone. The challenge to reach an understanding seemed to fascinate them, if only for a few minutes. I have little idea whether the version they arrived at was accurate. The accuracy seems to me considerably less important than the will to understand.

Of course, in another context the accuracy would be important. The text of the Mahabharata is sacred to Hindus. A Pakistani Moslem would not wish to be thought to look like an Indian god. As in so many aspects of work with young children, attention to the stage of understanding is important. We know that young children have little or no ability to distinguish between other places and other countries and have greatly simplified images of the third world (Scoffham 1999). The application of the 1999 Department for International Development (DfID) report on education and world citizenship is, therefore, complicated in their case. DfID themselves have given little emphasis to early years work in the implementation of the report, though some of the Development Education Centres (such as that in South Yorkshire) have encountered increasing demands on their assistance from early years services. I also suspect that young children's views of Africa as a hunter/gatherer economy may have as much to do with the fascination such a way of life holds for them as they take the first steps towards independence from the immediate family as it does with discriminatory images in the media.

I have spoken of the will to understand being more important than the accuracy of initial understanding. However, when staff in early years provision talk about training in equal opportunities they often speak as though what they feel is expected of them is detailed knowledge of the esoteric. The person offering training in special needs often has to clarify that it will be impossible to give detailed information on all the needs that might be encountered, that even children with the same specific syndrome will differ from each other. What is required is a readiness to deal with difference, to seek to understand, to cooperate with parents and child – principles that apply even in the case of children whose needs are not designated as 'special'.

The understanding of multicultural issues is also often discussed in terms of academically accurate knowledge of other cultures. This ignores the fact that changes inevitably occur to cultural identity once people are uprooted from the place where their culture was developed and moved somewhere else, especially now that many young black parents were themselves born in the United Kingdom. I have sometimes heard white staff say that they want to understand the origins and explanation of some custom relating to children common in one of the local minority communities. Yet they themselves can rarely offer a historical explanation of why white British people give chocolate eggs to children at Easter. If curiosity leads someone to seek out the answer to the question of how such customs arose, that is fair enough, but the real answer to the question is that 'We've always done it and it's fun'. That kind of explanation is not only one that connects the black and the white community in a shared understanding of the relationship between grown-ups and children, it is enchantingly less serious. The view that black people are not only different but are strange in ways that mean that understanding them is a matter of hard intellectual work is as big a barrier to mutual understanding as the notion that there are no differences at all (or would not be if minorities would come into line and support the English cricket team). All of us need to believe that it is worthwhile establishing fair relationships because there is bound to be some element of hard work in it. If the project is seen simply in terms of hard work and work that must be undertaken because of the requirements of the law or the childcare inspector, then no one is likely to take it seriously except as a nuisance.

The nature of the early years workforce creates some barriers to this kind of enterprise. The fact that it is overwhelmingly young, white, female and able-bodied means that it starts with the need to reach out to others and may be hampered in doing so because particular images of the world will be more readily reinforced in such a homogenous group. The Guidance for early years plans for the period 2001–4 specifies targets for attracting black people, men and people with disabilities into the childcare workforce. These targets supplement the work already in place at national and local level for general recruitment into early years care and education. The local partnerships are likely to run up against serious resource problems in undertaking this work. One of the issues is that most of the real opportunities for work-based training are with more mature staff, but the focus of the new Skills and Learning Council will be on those under 25. The lack of resources is not the only difficulty. Attitudes provide a more fundamental problem. The appointment of older people can be hampered by a mechanistic ascription of value to formal qualifications at appointment. The appointment of men creates problems because of suspicion of the motives of men entering a traditionally feminine preserve and because both sides often feel awkward in handling the reversal of traditional power relationships in one of the few contexts where women hold nearly all the positions of power and influence. The appointment of people with disabilities raises issues about whether they can be considered fit which point up the fact that 'fit person' judgements are often made in isolation rather than being seen in the context of the service provided and the role the person will have. The appointment of black people runs up against the fact that black and especially Asian people have chosen not to enter early years training on the scale they have been willing to enter other areas of health and social care training for reasons that need urgent research. There are also issues about the desire that they, like black parents coming into a unit, should provide a bridge between the largely white staff and black clientele – an idea that is usually well motivated but can overlook the fact that bridges are things that get walked over. There is also the risk of creating a segregated black service within the wider predominantly white one unless the black person's contribution is well planned within the total curriculum.

The problems are, therefore, many, but the development of a more broadly representative staff group is one of the strategies that providers can adopt in the effort to promote equality of opportunity.

If it is to be tackled properly, the issue of equal opportunities must be tackled with real seriousness rather than in a spirit of puritan gravity. It must be seen in terms of opening up new horizons for children and not of protecting them from discrimination or morally harmful influences alone. It must be seen in terms of ethical development rather than moral condemnation. It must be seen as a chance to discover new things rather than as an obligation to engage in difficult study of the obscure. It must be seen as integral to quality rather than some addition required by the law.

How does this affect the examination of this issue by childcare inspectors and how does such a perspective make this issue seem a little less intangible?

It is easier to say what childcare inspectors must not do.

They must not place undue reliance on formal statements of commitment to equal opportunities whether in the policy packs of providers or in dealing with assessments of suitability. In the early days of the Children Act there was something of a fashion for getting people to sign statements of their commitment. Where such statements formed parts of more general codes of conduct this was reasonable, but too much value was placed on separate statements. It was sometimes suggested that this created a new obligation and that it would be easier to deal with people who offended against equal opportunities because they had signed such scraps of paper. This was nonsense. Recourse to the piece of paper to be signed got childcare inspectors off the hook of testing out the nature of people's understanding and commitment for the time being. All that had happened was that the necessary assessment of attitude had been postponed from the relatively relaxed stage of registration assessment to the much more fraught context of inspection or investigation.

There is also little point in checking objects. Toys, books and pictures with images that are anti-stereotypical in nature will be part of a provider's equal opportunities policy only if there is clear understanding of their use. Too much emphasis on them can give the misleading impression that to possess them is all that is essential. Probably every childcare inspector has been confronted by a childminder holding out an 'ethnic' doll in a gesture reminiscent of someone in a horror film holding up a garlic-stained crucifix in the face of an advancing vampire. Besides, some of the 'equal opportunities' play material on the market is of dubious value: 'ethnic' dolls that are simply ordinary white dolls painted a different colour; kits for celebrating Divali seized upon eagerly in areas where most Asian people are Moslem; books that preach and others that make fun of sexist attitudes in ways that are more appealing to grown-ups than most young children ('and the princess did *not* get married and lived happily ever after', etc.). Those that are of value are not always easy to obtain. This is not to discourage efforts to develop anti-stereotypical images in a setting, simply to point out that it is more than a matter of shopping.

Statements and objects give little evidence at all. What does matter is practice and practice that avoids both the moral high ground and the search for detailed knowledge in the absence of immediate practical need. Malik (1998) offers a very useful practical guide for this area of the curriculum. The practice for which both providers and childcare inspectors should be looking is that which is at once open-minded and reflective, that seeks to broaden understanding and is prepared to recognise without guilt or defensiveness where there are barriers being created within the unit. It is practice that looks forward to things rather than fears what could go wrong.

Outdoor play

A playworker being interviewed for a research project said of children at her after-school club:

> They always have outdoor play – even in the winter, when it's dark. They don't *have* to go out but a lot of kids want to. Even if it's pouring with rain they want to go out. (Petrie 1994: 97)

and most early years workers will recognise the phenomenon. Bilton comments:

> Either young children are perverse, or in fact they instinctively know something which adults seem to have forgotten, namely that the outdoor is a natural learning and teaching environment for young children and one in which most children feel settled and capable. (Bilton 1998: vi)

When Stirling organised their Children as Partners project in their nurseries they found that demand for better outdoor provision was one of the priorities for their children (Kinney and McCabe 2001: 11).

Bilton points to the importance of outdoor play in pioneering work on nurseries in this country and how it linked with earlier playcare activity for slightly older children. She notes the decline in the importance attached to it and ascribes this to the increasingly exclusive emphasis from the late 1930s on the compensatory and care aspects of nursery provision and the failure to establish nursery provision as a field in its own right (Bilton 1998: 17–24). She might also have noted that in the minds of many in the first half of the 20th century outdoor play was connected with the wish to give children from overcrowded and unhealthy home environments access to fresh air, an objective that lost priority with the improvements to housing in the course of the century. By the 1960s the idea that children needed to be outside as much as possible to prevent diseases of the lung felt fairly quaint. Too many babies were thrown out with that particular bathful of water.

Whatever the reason for it, there was certainly a significant decrease until recently in the importance attached to outdoor play, though more particularly in day nurseries than in nursery education. A research team in the early 1980s could speak of the outside as 'the nearest a child gets to really "free" play' (Blatchford *et al.* 1982: 33). The assumption is interesting. At the time they wrote I was actively engaged in work on holiday playcare and would have seen the outside as the area that needed planning while the indoor space provided opportunity for individual self-directed relaxation. A decade later guidance issued by Hertfordshire's Education Department said that children aged three to five should have 'a daily routine which highlights outside play as an essential part of the provision, i.e. a minimum of half an hour a day' (Hertfordshire County Council Education Department 1991: 2). Those that constructed the guidance clearly thought that they were recognising the importance of outdoor activity, but they speak of half-an-hour a day. Admittedly, that is styled as a minimum, but even so...! Soon after the publication of that guidance the authors of the Midland Bank survey (which was conducted among nurseries that were probably better than average, if anything) 'observed some reluctance on the part of staff to use the outdoor area, and, when outside, they often tended to adopt a rather passive, overseeing role, not involving themselves directly with the children' (Vernon and Smith 1994: 63). Now things are beginning to alter, thanks to a considerable extent to the impact of Bilton's book, but also to other factors such as the bringing together of playworkers and pre-school workers in the local early years partnerships and some of the initiatives on local play policies that have followed from or been associated with parents' worries about the degeneration of local parks after the cuts of the 1980s. There is still, however, a long way to go and failings in that respect have sometimes been reinforced rather than corrected by the process of regulation. The Social Services Inspectorate discovered that 20 per cent of annual inspections under the Children Act in the local authorities they surveyed did not take outdoor play facilities into consideration (Social Services Inspectorate 2000: 48, Table 5).

In her explanation of the decline of focus on outdoor play, Bilton seems to me to pay insufficient attention to the need to give children access to 'fresh air' which dominated thinking in nursery care for a while. She also gives insufficient attention to the issue of safety. One of the major achievements of the 20th century was to bring about significantly increased safety in the home, partly through growing public awareness, but mainly through developments in design. The number of deaths and serious injuries of young children in the home in 1900 and the years that immediately followed was horrific. Improvement was steady for much of the century, but there was particular progress made in the housing of ordinary people in the 1960s and 1970s. As the home became safer, so the outside came to seem more dangerous. In some ways it *was* more dangerous. Increased traffic on the roads made them less and less safe as play areas even in quiet suburban cul-de-sacs. There was also a heightened awareness of other dangers because of media coverage. Although the number of deaths a year of children at the hands of strangers remained more or less constant in the last half of the 20th century, the coverage given to particular incidents helped to generate a view of the outside as threatening. The cramping effect on children's lives is recognised, but it is difficult to know how to tackle it. The parent worried about the traffic near her child's school is likely to take her child to school by car and thus add to the local traffic, contributing to an increasingly vicious cycle. Organised outdoor play activity in school holidays is an important compensatory measure, so important that we cannot allow the present situation to continue where the children of the more affluent have increasing access to such services offered on a commercial basis, but the community-based playschemes initiated in the 1970s in the poorer areas of town and country are in decline. At their best, however, organised playschemes are not enough. There is also the need to look again at outdoor play as an essential part of all early years services. The issue is one which is still not taken with sufficient seriousness.

Much of Bilton's book is taken up with demonstrating that it is possible to use the outdoors as a learning and teaching area, offering practical advice on how to set about it. She presents ideas about fundamental design and layout, including the advantages of the veranda as a means of facilitating a free flow between outside and inside play areas. This has helped to persuade many hesitant providers to try this approach and, finding success, they have gone on to integrate outdoor activity more thoroughly into their programmes. However, this leaves no real arguments in favour of outside play except the historical tradition and the evident eagerness of children themselves. If it is to seem worthwhile overcoming the fear of the outside and the disruption that changes of routine and arrangement entail, then there must be some consideration of the question of whether it might be impossible to offer adequate learning and teaching without outdoor activity.

One of the reasons why it is difficult to do this is that the subject is under-researched. Most research on child development has taken place under laboratory conditions, partly to secure the place of child psychology in the realm of science. This has a number of disadvantages in practice. Possibly the major one is that it fails to take adequately into account the interaction of child and carer in the course of the ordinary day. Almost as important is that it entails very few observations made outside. This is in spite of the fact that those working with young children are often aware of different behaviour patterns in the same child inside and outside. The possible need as well as desire of the young child for outside play is an issue little addressed in research.

We can dispense immediately with one version of why children need outside play. Bruce in her typology of ideas about play mentions without approval the idea that young children need to be rid of excess energy (Bruce 1991: 29–36). It is common to hear of the need for children to 'let off steam' as though, unlike older human beings, they produce another form of waste product. (Children themselves, picking up this half-disapproval of the grown-up world often speak of more boisterous forms of play as 'messing about'. Any born-again Freudian will spot the implications.)

There are, I think, four reasons why outside play is essential, though I readily accept that most of what I have to say is founded on intuition rather than research.

The first relates to the ability to understand spatial dimension. Our species did not evolve in buildings. For most of history the ability to understand the physical environment was connected with the fact that most of that environment was not man-made. It is interesting that we began in painting to develop ideas on perspective and the related matter of the use of light to suggest three-dimensional shape in the context of urban civilisation and in the period in which urbanism grew. Post-Renaissance oil painting was the first virtual reality. What happens in computers is merely an electronic speeding up of the effects. The built environment creates problems in the development of spatial ability which we have tackled partly through virtual reality. That tactic on its own may well be inadequate. What is seen within a box (the oil-painted canvas, the PC monitor) is focused and directed rather than opening up an unlimited range of spatial experience and demanding the development of skills in scanning, comparison making, measurement and choice of focus. Recent research on agoraphobia suggests that it may not be in most cases the consequence of emotional trauma, but rather a cognitive deficit, an inability to cope with a changing pattern of space that itself triggers anxiety and other negative emotions. Experience of the outside may thus be essential to intellectual ability (in spite of the image of the scholar crouched over a book in a dark study). The most fundamental mathematical capacities may depend on the experience at an early age of negotiating larger space.

The second relates to self-understanding and, in particular, the child's understanding of her own body. The outside offers a far richer range of opportunities for the child to understand her body and its capacities at a time when what Bruner calls the enactive aspect of learning is especially crucial (Bruner 1988). In a properly planned environment the outside may be a safer place for the child to experiment. Bilton provides a fascinating sketch of a visually impaired child making more confident use of the outdoor playspace at a nursery than many would think possible or safe (Bilton 1998, 62–3).

The outdoors presents more opportunities for children to create distance between themselves and their grown-up carers. It may be that not everyone sees this as an advantage. The greater difficulties of supervision outside explain why some staff feel the outside is worrying and why so many outside play areas are barren rectangular playgrounds with little intrinsic interest. In the slow path to independence this aspect of the outside is, however, crucial to many children.

The fourth way in which outside play is essential is that it is the best possible context for introducing children to an understanding of the physical environment, to ideas of seasons and the weather and to the living world. This is one of the things that makes design and layout so important. An outside play area that is simply a playground and entails no contact with plants, small creatures, a whole variety of textures and sensations is missing much of the point.

Of course, all the experiences described above can be replicated indoors by skilled early years workers. But such replications are often a poor substitute. This is the case even where the unit has a large indoor space available, perhaps especially then. It is far easier to generate a considerable amount of noise and confusion and risk of harm in a large hall with echoing sound than it is in an outside play area that is in fact smaller.

In spite of all that has been said, it remains true that many childcare inspectors are as nervous about the outside as many providers are. Because the learning opportunities of the outside are not recognised, the possibility of harm becomes the dominant consideration. This is especially true of the gardens of childminders which can contain more hazards than the minders' homes – steep drops, greenhouses, open water, sharp tools, chemicals, poisonous and spiky plants, easy access to the road, etc. Inspectors often suggest that people otherwise fit to be registered as minders should not be allowed to use their gardens, leaving the minder with the choice of not allowing children outside play at all or taking them to the local park where the outside space and the journey there may entail even more hazards than the garden, the use of which has been banned. Childcare inspectors whose own experience and expertise have been in work with the under-fives have often been baffled by playschemes whose premises are open spaces and bemused as to how they assess the safety of the equipment on an adventure playground. In the absence of a clear understanding of how serious an issue outside play is, childcare inspectors are tempted to look for what appears to be safe but may be damaging to children in the longer run.

This in turn raises two questions. There is a relatively easy one of whether the intelligent use of outside space should be one of the criteria by which providers are judged to be succeeding. Of course, it should. The more problematic question is whether providers should not be permitted to register if they are unable to provide direct access to appropriate open space. I am tempted to answer in the affirmative again, but this is obviously difficult in some instances, particularly in inner-city areas. Some local authorities have not registered people as childminders who live in flats because the lack of gardens makes outside play difficult, though also because of considerations relating to safe escape in emergency. Others have registered such people on condition that they come up with specific plans for providing outside play. The NDNA has argued strongly that immediately accessible outside playspace should not be an absolute requirement because that would lead to the closure of many existing nurseries, especially in London. On the other hand, the immediate availability of outside space has been made a requirement by regulators in some other European cities just as crowded as London. Rather than making an open-ended concession, this is, perhaps, one area where the Early Years Directorate should be insisting on action plans to rectify the lack of outside space even if the time scales for these are unusually generous. Anything less is going to give the wrong message about how serious an issue this is.

Music

Like outdoor play, music has been marginalised to some extent in early education. This is illustrated in the 1991 report from Her Majesty's Inspectorate on the teaching and learning of music in primary schools. They noted that 'Overall, policies for teaching music and planning work received less attention than most other subjects in the primary schools visited' (para. 20) and also that 'Music is more often taught by "specialist" teachers than any other subject in the primary years' (para. 72) and yet at the same time 'Not all schools have specialist music teachers' (para. 74). It is also interesting that most of their examples of good practice relate to children in years three, four, five or six, indicating a readiness to link good practice with the development of technical expertise by the children and the uncertainty as to the age at which children should be offered opportunities to acquire such expertise.

This is in spite or perhaps because of the fact that children are surrounded by a considerable quantity of ambient music and are likely to know not just nursery songs that have been specifically taught to them, but a wide range of TV theme tunes, pop songs and other snatches of music. The question is whether this familiarity can or should be harnessed to give music a more central place in early years services.

Music is the ideal medium for teaching the idea of order while reinforcing the perception that order is compatible with both change and pleasure. This is the fundamental notion that underpinned the place music had in all educational activity for many centuries. It may be less common today, but it is still a concept that has relevance for the very serious matter of scientific advance. Speaking of his major breakthrough in thinking about physics in 1905 Einstein said:

> It occurred to me by intuition and music was the driving force behind that intuition. My discovery was the result of musical perception. (quoted in Fryer 1985: 42)

Some might see this as the eccentricity of genius, but others have made large claims for music in the development of normal skills. Atarah Ben-Tovim writes:

> There is only one occupation open to most children which offers the possibility of developing mind, body and soul in balance: learning to play an instrument. (Ben-Tovim 1979: 11)

Ben-Tovim was talking primarily about school-age children. There is some evidence of the importance of music in child development at the earliest stage. For example, while adults in all cultures engage in particular types of speech when interacting with babies, the features of 'baby-talk' vary from culture to culture. The one common feature appears to be the use of a distinctive pitch (Fernald 1989). Some have made extensive claims for the centrality of skills closely linked to music making and appreciation in early development (Wisbey 1980, see especially pp. 9–10).

The pleasure, excitement and comfort young children derive from music is well documented and is one of the reasons why it is likely to be an effective aid to learning in several ways, including especially ideas of structure and the experience of working together. Although nearly all young children are accustomed to hearing or making music, it is still not common for serious efforts to be made to work with them on listening to music. This is in spite of the fact that access to a wide range of recorded music has never been easier. There was a great deal of excitement a short time ago when it was observed that babies seemed to have a strong preference for Mozart. The idea that there is a natural disposition to attend to 'serious' music cheered up those who felt that such tastes were being overwhelmed by factory-produced pop. It seems likely that the real attraction of Mozart is to do with the fact that his period fell between the baroque period in music (in which rhythm was more clearly marked and transitions between movements more dramatic) and the romantic (with its complex narrative or programmatic structures). His music has a structure that may be in some ways easier for them to absorb because of the way it avoids the extremes of those two periods. The fact that recordings of some of his music are now being used extensively with very young children will probably have a reinforcing effect. Sounds that are familiar are comforting even when they lack the charm of Mozart. It would be unusual for a baby to be soothed to sleep by the music of Jimi Hendrix or of Stockhausen, but it would not be surprising if the child's parents had a fondness for them and played recordings of them frequently. What is clear is that young children can be helped by listening to a wide range of music and need not be confined to children's songs. The imaginative use of music to listen to is one of the striking features of the pre-school education in Reggio Emilia in Italy.

The very concept of a child's song is a comparatively recent invention of Western Europe. It is one aspect of the invention of childhood. In most cultures music is segregated, if at all, in terms of gender rather than age. This is because music has often been an aid to work, establishing rhythms in societies where people rather than machines engaged in repetitive tasks, and work has often been gender specific. Music as an aid to work is much better established as a practice in nurseries than serious listening. The use of singing, body percussion sounds and rhythmic movement to underpin other learning activity is the one example of widespread music practice. It has a long history. Before the mass production of recorded sound, singing was the only cheap way of introducing music to pre-school settings and remains important.

The question is whether it is possible in music making to go further than singing or the use of simple instruments. It is at this point that the subject of music connects with a whole series of controversies about pre-school education. It is a particular example of the broader question of how technical skills should be introduced. There are three broad kinds of consideration that influence practice here.

Some would emphasise that young children need to gain confidence in their own problem solving, so that it is important to accept their approaches to problems rather than to ensure that they arrive at the best possible solution. The process is more important than the product. In terms of music making this suggests the need to allow the children's own patterns to emerge in performing, composing and instrument making. To focus on greater technical competence is to risk undermining the confidence and interest of children. Against this there is the success that has been attained by the followers of Kodaly and Suzuki in teaching very young children to play instruments to a high level of skill and the fact that – contrary to the expectations of many – the children do not seem oppressed by this experience. There is similar experience in relation to drawing in China where high levels of skill have been encouraged in young children by direct teaching and they have sometimes used these skills in ways that have surprised their own teachers (Cox 1992: 183–8. See especially p. 187).

This leads to consideration of a second factor – that approaches to the arts are still governed to a large extent by romantic notions of the inspired performer who needs to break away from the deadening prison of technique. In the 19th century, Romanticism in all its aspects was a necessary revolt against conventions that had become restricting rather than helpful. Taken to extremes the attitudes it generated conceal the fact that inspiration is only possible once technical competence is achieved and there are tools to be used for expression. All too often we have a fundamentally ambivalent attitude to children's 'art' work. They are encouraged, for example, to experiment with paint and colour. The results are then pinned up with no context suggesting what is being learned, as though the paintings were finished products on display in an art gallery. We refrain from teaching simple drawing skills, but praise the child that produces a picture which (often by accident as much as effort) has strong realist characteristics or a real sense of movement or effective overall structure. We get away with that ambivalence in visual art because young children are naturally drawn to play with material that produces a final visible effect. The ambivalence is more undermining in the case of music.

The third factor is the perception that music making is terribly difficult. Together with maths and art it is one of those things that grown-ups (including some early years staff) will cheerfully acknowledge they cannot do. Many will claim to be tone deaf. Tone deafness is a real but very rare phenomenon. What those who lay claim to it usually mean is that they have had bad learning experiences which need to be put right in their case and prevented in the case of the children with whom they are concerned. The idea that musical performance (or even musical appreciation) is very difficult makes the complexity of the technical something disabling and alienating rather than an opportunity for mastery.

What should be done by any early years setting that wished to take music seriously, that is to say, treat it as a source of real enjoyment and learning?

Given the attitudes and hesitations that many staff will bring to the subject, there are good reasons for introducing a music specialist into the setting. There are also dangers and the work of such a specialist must be seen as an integral part of the work of the setting and not as an add-on if it is to be truly effective.

There will be an exploration of a wide range of music and not just of song associated with young children. There will be experiment to see what forms of music children like (their tastes will often surprise). Music from other countries can be used to provide rhythmic backing to activity, opening up aspects of the wider world and providing yet another element to a multicultural approach.

The question of technical skill will be tackled in ways that are attentive to children's development. This is particularly important in the area of musical notation. There is a tendency to two extremes – to leave it until later because it is so difficult or to teach it in a spirit of grim determination because it is so difficult. We have developed sophist-icated thinking about the foundations of literacy that is scarcely matched in the case of representing sound. Writers on the subject such as Phillips (1979: 29–65) and Dankworth (1984: 246–8) have developed ideas on introductory forms of musical notation, but have not attracted the attention they deserve.

Staff and parents can be involved as learners alongside the children. If the grown-ups have a limited understanding of music, there is no reason why that should not be acknowledged. Grown-ups who learn alongside children can take greater pleasure in the children's progress if the area of skill is not a mystery to them. Children can realise from seeing grown-ups learn that learning is a lifetime occupation and not something just for children. The very fact that musical performance and even some types of listening are seen as difficult can be turned to advantage.

Finally, where young children wish to, they can be helped to develop significant technical competence in performance by people who know how to teach such skills. The fact that grown-ups are sometimes a little scared of the demands of such learning should not become an impediment to children who wish to achieve it. There is plenty of evidence from history that children can achieve significant skill in this field because their minds are more alert to structure. The problem with child prodigies in the past has come from their exploitation as performers, not from the serious work entailed in acquiring skill.

A provider that developed a music strategy with elements such as those above may well attract praise from a childcare inspector. The failure to develop such strategies is unlikely to be the subject of adverse comment – simply because such a failure repres-ents the more usual situation. We need to reconsider the priorities implicit in that. The enjoyment to be derived from music is enormous, but it will be constrained unless the issue is taken seriously.

Conclusion

As I said in opening this chapter, the four topics were chosen because they seemed to me to illustrate some fundamental confusions. What is important is seen as serious in the sense of being grave. The question of how to protect from harm is examined in isolation from other issues in ways that inhibit proper risk assessment and can lead to unnecessary caution by both providers and inspectors. That focus, rather than giving them opportunities to learn, leads to a splitting up of aspects of quality that makes the proper assessment of each element more problematic. At best this means that regula-tion is reduced to particular aspects of quality on some of which the childcare inspectors may be accepted as expert. At worst it leads to tension between the demands of the regulator on the one hand and of educationists and the children themselves on the other. Once again fragmentation undermines the effectiveness of the work and the regulatory system contributes to rather than helps to overcome that fragmentation.

Chapter 6
Does regulation work?

Introduction

In the first two chapters I outlined the history of early years and their regulation up to the point at which preparations started to launch the Early Years Directorate. The next three chapters dealt with different aspects of how regulation might operate. However, they left to one side a more fundamental question. Do we need a system of early years regulation at all?

Some have questioned how useful the system we have had has been in practice. In the 1970s their research led the Jacksons to conclude that there was no difference in quality between registered and unregistered minders overall (Jackson and Jackson 1979: 95). It might be said that that was in the bad old days before the Children Act. However, legislative change did not produce any immediate change of mind in Sonia Jackson. In the excellent book on day care for the under-threes that she wrote with Elinor Goldschmied regulation hardly figures at all as a subject and when it does the tone is slighting:

> ... inspection on its own will neither create new services nor provide quality in those that exist. Our discussions with organisers of private nurseries suggest that it is more likely to produce severe irritation. (Goldschmied and Jackson 1994: 6)

It is true that their quarrel appears to have been mainly with the Conservative Government then in power which sought to leave the development of early years services to market forces with regulation offering some kind of defence against bad practice that might be concealed from parents. Nevertheless, it is difficult for a child-care inspector not to be antagonised by such a comment.

I have no argument with the idea that inspection alone will not produce quantity or quality in early years services. Did anyone ever expect it to? For that matter any one initiative that might be seen as important – improved training and professional development, significant increases in resources, better coordination and planning or whatever

– will not be capable *on its own* of transforming the early years scene. At best regulation will always be a citizen, not the king, in the realm of effort to improve services.

I also accept that some providers will find inspection severely irritating. But what is the significance of that in any particular case? A provider might be irritated because the childcare inspector had behaved in an officious manner or because a comfortable routine had been subject to the disturbing impact of outside scrutiny and the realisation that there was still room for improvement or because a requirement had been imposed that an essential but expensive safety measure be adopted. What we make of the provider's irritation in any one case depends considerably on the precise reason for it. In evaluating the effectiveness of any regulatory regime we always have to distinguish between what is required by regulation and the manner in which it is required. There are often cases when the former is reasonable and the latter is not.

We have little research evidence on the benefits of regulation in the field of early years, especially in the form it has taken since 1991. Save the Children and the Thomas Coram Research Unit have given us useful pictures of what happened in the first phase of Part X's implementation (Petrie 1995; Candappa *et al.* 1996), but their work is more descriptive than evaluative. Apart from the Social Services Inspectorate (2000) report few have tried since then to assess the impact of the new form of regulation or the advantages and disadvantages of the different approaches taken in different local authorities. All statements on the usefulness of regulation must include an element of educated guesswork, even of faith.

My personal inclination is to believe that regulation is worthwhile in principle and has gone some way to demonstrating its usefulness in practice. The reader is entitled to think that I would say that; as someone earning my living in that sphere, it is only natural that I should come to such a conclusion. A more important criticism that could be made of my initial response to the question is that it rests on impressions. I can think of a large number of examples where regulation has been successful in improving or reinforcing quality and preventing – or at worst dealing speedily with – problems that have emerged. Yet it is difficult to base very much on anecdote except where this gives clearer shape to conclusions based on more systematically gathered evidence. I could also think of examples of failure and weighing up the lessons of anecdotes with conflicting implications is an impossible task.

Examples of regulation producing worthwhile effects in particular circumstances could be seen as more significant if it could be agreed that there have been significant advances in the quality of early years services in the period since Part X of the Children Act was implemented. Many would argue that there has been such an improvement over the past decade. However, the impression that there has been such a development, even if widely shared, does raise a number of questions. At the most fundamental level it can and should be asked: what precisely is meant by saying that things are better? Some have questioned whether expansion in day care was a good thing at all, arguing that greater freedom of choice for parents has been won at the expense of children. Others who are in favour of day care as long as it is of high quality might suggest that the continued fragmentation of the system of provision detracts too seriously from the quality of what is provided to be ignored and add that regulation is part of the policy package that has bolstered fragmentation. Others have questioned whether the priorities being assigned to different aspects of quality are well judged and blamed regulation for distortions in the setting of priorities.

It could also be asked whether childcare inspectors who assert that they can see improvements are talking about real improvements in quality or simply greater skill on the part of providers in surviving inspection. This is a question that was raised in relation to Annex A on improvement in the quality of provision in OFSTED's review of the first year of the inspection regime operating as part of the Nursery Grant Scheme (OFSTED 1998: 17). The more doubts there are about the validity of the ways in which quality is measured by childcare inspectors, the more pertinent such questions become.

Even if we can agree on what 'better' means and can agree that there is evidence that what we now have is better than the situation that existed ten years ago, the question of how regulation has contributed to this remains to be addressed. I said earlier that no one factor on its own could guarantee improvement. There are many factors that have made for improvement in the recent past. These include changing expectations in society in general, the consolidation of a body of professional opinion and the specific provisions for support to services made under the National Childcare Strategy. It can be argued that even in the absence of regulation these would have led to major improvements.

The view from abroad

One way of approaching the question is to examine the experience of other developed countries. This does not take us very far because the particular type of regulatory regime we have is, in fact, something of a rarity. Where regulation exists in other countries it tends to operate in more direct ways than here. That is to say, regulation either informs the way that the services offered directly by the state are governed or it informs the basis on which services are offered at the behest of public authorities and constitutes part of a system of contract compliance. The idea of a state agency that checks the independently organised services provided to parents is not unique to the UK, but neither is it a model that many other countries have.

The USA provides a contrasting example in a number of ways. In 1968 the Federal Interagency Day Care Requirements (FIDCR) were issued, specifying standards for levels of staff training, health and safety, parent involvement, staff:child ratios and available space in premises. Although the term 'requirements' was used, the standards were not imposed except in so far as non-compliance was made grounds for denying federal funds. There was also no specific inspectorate created, although the document spoke of 'periodic evaluation'. Each federal agency administering a programme where FIDCR applied was responsible for enforcement and this does not seem to have happened consistently. The regulations themselves were considered for revision several times and always in an atmosphere of heated debate. There was a running conflict between those who wanted to promote childcare as a way of helping women back to work and, therefore, wanted to keep restrictions on providers to a minimum and those, on the other hand, who sought to ensure the highest possible quality of the childcare that was available out of a belief that this would be a better long-term investment in the nation's future. In the debate, existing requirements came to have an iconic status for many practitioners in the field so that any suggestion they be revised was seen as an abandonment of quality. There is a detailed account of what happened in Nelson (1982). The personalities and the institutional arrangements are quite different but there is much that is reminiscent of the debate in this country in 2000 on the proposed new National Standards.

The Republican Party was always wary of state intervention and regulation in this sphere, seeing it as unwarranted interference with the rights of parents. In 1981 President Reagan abolished FIDCR and gave responsibility for the design and enforcement of regulation to the individual states. They, for the most part, proved even less active than the federal agencies. Similar devolution of regulatory responsibility also occurred in Canada, with consequent wide variation between the provinces. According to one commentator, the principal consequence of deregulation was not an overall decline in standards so much as a decline in the quality of care available to children from low-income families (Clarke-Stewart 1991: 39). She draws the conclusion that regulation should be focused on enforcing minimum standards to protect the very poor rather than on the promotion of quality in general (p. 59), a view related to the positive role she ascribes to day care as a compensatory measure. A similar line is taken by Morgan (1984) who also spells out the measures she feels are needed in addition to regulation in the strictest sense to ensure quality in provision. The arguments put forward by Clarke-Stewart suggest a quite different approach to the issue of how regulation should be conducted from the one that I have taken in this book. However, there is a distinction to be made between the consequences of deregulation that she and others have observed in recent North American history and the practical conclusions that can be drawn from those observations. I have no reason to doubt the accuracy of the observations themselves. It does not follow that regulatory action must be targeted in as narrow a way as she suggests. The prevention of the worst practice is partly achieved by the prevention of practice that is not as good as it might be and that in turn is achieved more effectively by the promotion of good practice than by mere policing.

In looking at the American experience we also need to bear in mind the differences between the American system of public services and our own. Deregulation in the sense of abandoning national legislation and systems of enforcement in order to empower more devolved levels of government is something that has also been tried in Sweden and Spain, often held up as models of early years practice, as well as in other European Union countries such as Austria. In Sweden it has been claimed that this form of deregulation has led to some decline in standards in some specific respects, whereas in Spain some of the communities having devolved powers, such as Catalonia or the city of Madrid, have used those powers to raise local standards above the minimum required (McGurk *et al.* 1995: 6–7). As Morgan claims and the Spanish and

Italian examples seem to prove, a great deal depends on the public and political will to develop high-quality services. Denmark has little in the way of regulation, but there is such heavy investment in early years services that standards appear to be higher than they are in countries where much more prescriptive regulation operates (McGurk *et al.* 1995: 25).

Once again the experience of other countries demonstrates that it is possible to do things differently to the way we do them here, but that it would be rash to draw any immediate conclusion from such evidence as to the best possible way of doing things. Much depends on the cultural and political context. In the USA the abandonment of federal regulation was part of a politically driven emphasis on family responsibility and seems to have backfired for those families that struggled to meet their responsibilities. In some parts of Spain and Italy at least it has facilitated improvement where politicians wanted it. We need to consider our own cultural and political context and how that bears on the issue.

The situation in the UK

The idea of regulation by inspection is well established in the UK. There are many examples of regulation provided by public authorities intervening to protect the safety of consumers or employees in what are essentially private contractual arrangements and of the general public in relation to the environment. The concept has its roots in the 19th century, in the great public health reforms and the development of the factory schools inspectorates. Concern at particular incidents often leads to new regulation, one of the most recent examples being the Dangerous Dogs Act, an example that also illustrates the potential danger of legislation being drafted in the context of moral panic, since it is often poorly framed, as most would now agree that particular Act of Parliament was. Our tradition of regulation is a frequent source of misunderstanding with some of our partners in the European Union who bring to agreement on standards, for example in relation to the environment, a tradition in which legislation is often seen in terms of agreed aspiration rather than the enforcement of those standards by adequately resourced regulatory agencies.

The fact that we have a well-established approach to the use of regulation in tackling problems in this country gives that approach the advantage of familiarity. People are prepared to use and to respect regulatory regimes because such practice is part of the national culture. (One of the issues with which OFSTED has had to come to terms in the establishment of the Early Years Directorate is the amount of time childcare inspectors spend on investigation – and sometimes mediation – as opposed to routine inspection and the extent to which this is a response to public demand that will not easily go away.) On the other hand, the fact that it is well established does not make it sacrosanct. If other developed nations have not seen the need for it, is it as vital as those engaged in it normally assume?

Part of the difficulty in answering that question is that regulation is a relatively under-theorised area in legal studies in spite of the prevalence of regulation by inspection in much of British law. It is significant that recent editions of such standard texts as Keenan (1995), Barker and Padfield (1992) and Redmond and Shears (1995) do not have even index references to regulation let alone chapters or sections specifically on the subject. We lack a thoroughgoing body of principles on which individual decisions can be based. Where issues have come before the courts and it has not been possible to resolve them quickly by reference to specific sections of regulatory statute, magistrates and judges have employed general principles in combination with their own understanding of what would be reasonable in the precise circumstance. The fact that relatively few cases relating to Part X have come before the High Court means there is little in the way of legal precedent. The freedom of the lower courts to consider matters afresh remains unfettered. (In this respect the regulation of early years services is in a different situation from some other areas where considerably more litigation has taken place.)

The attitude of the courts has led some childcare inspectors to feel undermined since decisions arrived at by proper administrative process have not necessarily been upheld. Attempts by Family Proceedings Courts and the High Court to be even-handed in their comments on providers and inspectors have been seen as undermining the authority of the inspectors. It should be clear from the comments I made in Chapter 2 that this is not a view with which I have much sympathy myself. The possibility of ill-considered officer action makes it necessary for the courts to examine how decisions have been made and they have ruled correctly in distinguishing between statute and official guidance. The decision to refer appeals under Part VI of the Care Standards Act to the Tribunal being established under the Protection of Children Act might suggest to some childcare inspectors that their professional judgements are now more likely to be upheld, since they will be considered by a more specialist body. This will not necessarily be the case and the strengthening of the regulatory regime produced by the new appeals procedure is likely to prove ill-founded if the concerns shared by the Early Years Directorate and the Tribunal are not shared in the same way by providers, parents and others with a stake in the early years field. The strong possibility of the Human Rights Act 1998 being invoked against decisions of the Early Years Directorate and the Tribunal remains and some decisions could come under judicial review. There are and must be limits to the powers of any regulatory regime even when the interests of potentially vulnerable children are at issue, precisely to ensure that steps taken to protect children are well-considered ones.

A further complication in the national picture is that the previous Conservative Government made regulation such a high-profile political issue. For them it became a matter of principle to deregulate as far as possible. They had a distaste for the kind of conformity associated with regulation, but their principle objection was to the cost to the provider. Regulation always entails such costs – both the cost of bringing the product up to required standards and costs associated with cooperation with both general regulation such as that arising from the Asylum and Immigration Act 1996 or regulation specific to the type of activity in which a business is engaged. The cost of cooperating with the regulatory process has probably been a nuisance rather than a real hindrance to providers of early years services so far. However, costs associated with conforming to the requirements of the Protection of Children Act could prove prohibitive for many community organisations, creating a kind of tax on volunteering. This is an issue on which many voluntary organisations including the PLA have expressed concern.

The stance of the Conservative Government on deregulation has in some respects been followed by the present one. The proposed National Standards issued in the summer of 2000 were a concession to private enterprise that went beyond even the demands of private enterprise itself. At around the same time the Better Regulation Unit of the Cabinet Office produced the 'Enforcement Concordat' which laid down a number of principles that should inform the actions of regulatory regimes, including openness, helpfulness, proportionality and consistency.

In practice the limits to deregulation have been set by two types of consideration. One is the gravity of the possible consequences of unregulated trading. If I buy a hi-fi set that is not fit for the purpose, a robust free marketeer could see this as just my problem. If I buy a car that is not fit for the purpose, I could kill not just myself but other people. The other consideration is that of the degree of expertise needed to assess a product. A consumer can make choices based on appearances and personal taste, but may lack the technical competence to make judgements on fitness for purpose and seek the security of knowing that a regulator has imposed certain standards. It is easy enough to judge that you prefer a particular brand of chocolate biscuit, another to assess the design work that has gone into a machine or a software programme.

Both these considerations apply to the care and education of young children. The deaths or abuse of children in some settings have demonstrated how badly wrong things can go when regulation slips. They pose the question of what would happen without regulation. Morgan (1984: 163–4) asserts that disastrous incidents as well as a broader decline in standards followed from deregulation in the United States. While parents and other carers can gain an impression of a setting from visits, they may not know what to look for and may be responsive to a friendly welcome and bright decoration. This is especially true since effective choice is very limited for most parents. The Midland Bank Survey illustrated many of the problems that parents have in making real choices when it comes to childcare (Vernon and Smith 1994). Such considerations are reinforced by the surges of public opinion in favour of tighter control that surface at the time of particular incidents. A 1995 *Panorama* programme, prompted by one accidental death and showing how badly things could go wrong in early years services probably did much to dampen down any inclination on the part of John Major's Government to weaken regulation in this field. There is, nevertheless, a significant body of opinion seeking to limit the scope of early years regulation to the prevention of significant harm. Such views are often associated with the '*laissez-faire*' approach which was among the four broad approaches to general policy on children and their families identified by Fox Harding (1997: 109–56).

What would happen if early years regulation were to be abolished?

There is a further complication in all this. The issue is not just whether early years services should be regulated, but whether they should have a specific regulatory regime. The abolition of Part X of the Children Act and the non-implementation of Part VI of the Care Standards Act would not leave early years services unregulated, simply without a regulatory regime of their own. If there were no childcare inspectors as such, the remaining agencies would need to review their practice, but such a drastic step would not leave children and their families completely without protection.

Responsibility for health and safety issues is already shared with the fire and rescue service and also with the local authority environmental health services which have had particular responsibilities for premises used for childcare under the Health and Safety at Work Act since 1998 and have responsibilities under other legislation, including the Food Hygiene Regulations Act 1990. Planning departments also have responsibilities in some circumstances under the Building Regulations Act 1958 and the Disability Discrimination Act 1995. These agencies, environmental health in particular, might need to modify their style of operation and take a more proactive stance in relation to providers if childcare inspection as such were abolished, since it is frequently on the initiative of childcare inspectors that they become involved in the first place. They would also need to develop more specific expertise in relation to the needs of young children than they necessarily have at present. Such changes in practice and training might be problematic but they would not be impossible. In other words, responsibility for premises and related issues such as catering could be passed entirely back to those that had it when responsibility for implementing the 1948 Act was transferred to the new social services departments.

Primary responsibility for the protection of children from abuse is in the hands of the social services departments and a number of other agencies. The disappearance of childcare inspection would mean that child protection staff no longer had the assistance of childcare inspectors in their dealings with early years settings with which many of them are still unfamiliar. There would also be a case for proactive intervention by the departments to ensure that providers were adhering to the provisions of the Protection of Children Act 1999. That is something that would have resource implications on a significant scale. However, the system of child protection in early years settings does not have to depend on the existence of a regulatory regime specific to those settings. It could be based on a readiness to take those issues more seriously and develop particular expertise in relation to them.

Broader issues of quality could also have some form of regulation. In 1999 OFSTED made clear to local authorities in a series of regional meetings that the existence of the system for inspecting providers under the Nursery Grant Scheme did not remove their power or responsibility to decide whether or not they wanted to use the services of all providers with eligible status. Contract compliance remained in the hands of the purchasers. The Nursery Grant Scheme affects only three- and four-year-olds, but local early years partnerships assist providers with access to funding in a variety of ways and could make such funding dependent on conformity to agreed standards. This would be a system of regulation similar to that in some other countries where funding decisions rather than inspection provide the means of enforcement. There would be problems with such an approach. It would, for example, undermine the principle of partnership if individual providers were being held to account more systematically by the partnerships, which would probably mean in practice by the education departments. However, such problems are always there when funding is distributed and partnerships would have to face it whatever was decided about regulation by some other agency.

There is also the role of accreditation regimes to consider. The more recognition such schemes receive, the more the status associated with them will be needed and the more its absence will be seen as a disadvantage. There comes a point at which an atmosphere creating the expectation of certain behaviour does not feel very different from compulsion determined by the law. Quality assurance could become a more significant way of ensuring adhesion to a wide range of standards, not just those directly linked to safety, in the absence of a childcare inspectorate.

The picture I have sketched of what things would be like without a childcare inspectorate is not, I think, implausible. It might cause alarm to some, but it is possible to imagine such a system functioning, although it would require significant investment in both staffing and training by the other agencies that have a role in the protection of children from accidental or deliberate harm. The fundamental question is whether we want more than such a system could offer.

Conclusion

One thing is evident. The minimal merely protective role of childcare inspection could be achieved without a specific regulatory regime if other regulatory bodies adapted their own operations to meet the needs that would be created by the absence of childcare inspection as such. Therefore a specific regulatory regime can only be justified if the role is greater than one of protecting children from significant harm, if it is also a mechanism for the promotion of quality in its broadest sense.

Thus the approach described in earlier chapters, an approach in which consideration is given to the whole spectrum of quality issues and in which the regulatory process has a strong supportive element is not a matter of choice or personal inclination. It is the only basis on which a specific childcare inspectorate can be justified and, therefore, operate in a coherent way.

To say this is not to say that such a service is essential. It could be regarded as a luxury. The question then becomes whether we are content with a minimum for children or want in some sense or another to do better than that.

Chapter 7
Conclusion

My answer to the question posed at the end of the last chapter would be a positive one. I want to see neither the deregulation of early years services nor the restriction of the scope of such services to efforts to protect children from significant harm. I want regulation to be part of the struggle to achieve the best possible day care and education services for young children. That does not imply that the standards to be imposed on services should be the highest that can be imagined.

One reason for this is that there cannot be absolute certainty about the components of quality. The idea of quality is one based on values and experience and both change and develop over time. The more attention we pay to ideas about quality in other countries (not just the most developed nations, but others also), the more the potential for change will be there. It would be foolish to suggest that anyone could determine the criteria of quality in early years services for more than the short term.

Another reason is that the highest is not necessarily the best. Indeed, there is some evidence that what appear at first to be higher standards can be associated with adverse effects. McGurk *et al.* (1995: 23) quote one kind of example. Another is where ambitious forms of recording make requirements beyond the capacity of staff and lead to less effective recording than simpler systems might have produced. There is tension between the search for efficiency in design and the achievement of effective design, between aspiration and what is immediately possible. Setting quality standards at a level at which all but the best provision would become unviable is not necessarily in children's interests. The alternatives to the provision that regulation had killed off might be even less desirable. However, the tension is not one to be managed primarily in terms of compromise between conflicting demands. (The experience of FIDCR in the United States shows how dangerous that can be.) It is rather a matter of appreciating that quality is a developmental matter, not just in the sense that our ideas about it change all the time, but that any good provider is in a constant search for improvement, aspiring to increasingly higher standards. If a provider is good in that sense (and many are), then quality will be promoted by supporting them in developing it rather than punishing them for failure.

Thus the 'best possible' is not the same as 'the best we can imagine'. It is, nevertheless, more than the minimalist interpretation of the deregulators or even that of those who wish to focus on the prevention of harm.

In other words, the argument I put forward is one for regulation of significant scope and ambition. I would not argue that regulation to secure higher standards is needed because good quality early years services can have an absolutely decisive impact on children's development and reverse what was being called a quarter-of-a-century ago the cycle of deprivation. The evidence for such a position seems to me as fuzzy as the evidence for the often opposing position that day care is damaging or at best a necessary evil in certain situations. The case that childcare should have a central position in strategies for social and economic regeneration still has to be made in detail, although that is no reason for the casual dismissal of it in the male-dominated bodies that often have responsibility for regeneration programmes.

I argue that we need a childcare inspection regime that seeks more than minimum standards simply because an increasing number of children are spending an increasing amount of time in early years services and we owe it to them to ensure that they are as good as possible. The beneficial consequences of making them excellent may be a matter for controversy. The appalling consequences of putting up with second or third best are evident. Effort, including regulation, to make services better is the best possible defence against them degenerating in much the same way as the protection of children from abuse is only effective when such activity is an integral part of an overall system of family support.

What does this imply about the ways in which childcare inspectors approach their work? It implies that the childcare inspector must:

* see her work as an integral part of the national and local childcare and education strategies;
* play an active part in the devising of concepts of quality and the criteria by which it is to be measured and not be content to impose standards received from above;
* be engaged in continuing reflection on the operation of the regulatory regime with colleagues in the immediate team and beyond;
* be engaged in continuing dialogue with others who are making contributions to the development of quality, including those from other regulatory agencies, providers and their staff, support and development workers, those engaged in training and professional development and those with responsibility for coordination and the allocation of resources in the partnerships;
* consider the field as a whole as well as individual settings in a comprehensive manner, seeking to learn how each aspect of a situation relates to every other one;
* consider both the field and individual settings in a developmental perspective, looking at the potential for change and not merely at what is observed at a particular moment in time;
* approach assessments in a supportive way wherever possible, starting with an assumption of shared fundamental values unless and until it becomes clear that this is not the case;

- be prepared to recommend enforcement in an informed and assertive manner, avoiding timidity on the one hand and hasty recourse to the use of power on the other;
- seek in so far as this is practicable the active involvement of all those with an interest in any assessment, including providers, their staff, the children, parents or other carers and advisory or development workers;
- conduct assessments in a reflective manner, considering her own approach to observation and judgement, taking into account the impact of her intervention on the setting;
- report on findings and make recommendations in ways that are clear not only within the regulatory regime but also to providers and their clientele.

All this is in line with the four propositions of which I spoke in the introductory chapter.

The fragmentation of early years services, which has been reinforced in several respects by earlier regulatory regimes, is a barrier to their effective development. Whatever the merits of the Government's current cautious and pragmatic approach to integration, seeking consensus on values and partnership in delivery of services rather than pushing for greater institutional change, the need in the longer term to bring the long struggle against fragmentation to a successful conclusion remains. The precise form a more integrated approach to early years services would require is something on which we still need to work. Shared values are to be created almost as much as they are to be discovered and childcare inspectors have a part to play in that.

Regulation must be about the promotion of quality in its broadest sense. The need to avoid harm has always been the bottom line in regulation. It is a line that needs to be drawn firmly. An exclusive focus on it is self-defeating. We need to become more ambitious for the sake of the children with whom and on behalf of whom we are working.

Assessment of quality must be a matter of examining the setting as a whole, taking into account the full range of welfare and educational issues, the context in time and place and the ways in which it might develop rather than a matter of attempting to measure the extent to which a setting meets specific criteria.

Objectivity in the conduct of regulation is not to be equated with detachment. There are limits to the extent to which techniques of detachment contribute to objectivity in regulation as in research. The childcare inspector needs to be reflective about her own practice and to examine where distance is or is not useful. Given the genuine commitment to what is best for children held by most of those engaged in the field, regulation must be conducted wherever possible in cooperation, actively involving all those, including the children, that have an interest in the matter, being ruthlessly honest where such cooperation is made impossible by negligence or abuse or the risk of either. This is important to make assessment in a regulatory context as accurate as possible. It is also the only way to prevent regulation becoming a marginalised activity with little or no job satisfaction.

It has been as difficult in the writing of this book as it often is in the process of regulation itself to keep children at the centre of the picture. That is, however, where they belong. Efficient administration and clear criteria are essential parts of any regulatory system, but must not be allowed to overshadow what is the central issue, the quality of the child's experience. Any system of childcare inspection that is going to be really worth having must be an integral part of the process of opening up as many opportunities as possible for them. Achieving that is the primary challenge that faces the Early Years Directorate as it takes on its task.

Bibliography

Aboud, F. (1988) *Children and Prejudice*. Oxford: Basil Blackwell.

Anning, A. and Edwards, A. (eds) (1999) *Promoting Children's Learning from Birth to Five: Developing the Early Years Professional*. London: Open University Press.

Astington, J. W. (1994) *The Child's Discovery of the Mind*. London: Fontana Press.

Barker, D. L. A. and Padfield, C. F. (1992) *Law*, 8th edn. Oxford: Butterworth-Heinemann Ltd.

Ben-Tovim, A. (1979) *Children and Music*. London: Adam and Charles Black.

Bilton, H. (1998) *Outdoor Play in the Early Years: Management and Innovation*. London: David Fulton Publishers.

Blatchford, P. *et al.* (1982) *The First Transition: Home to Pre-school*. Windsor: Nelson in association with the National Foundation for Educational Research.

Blenkin, G. and Kelly, V. (2000) 'The concept of infancy – a case for reconstruction', *Early Years: An International Journal of Research and Development* **20**(2), 30–38.

Bloch, F. and Buisson, M. (1998) *La garde des énfants une histoire de femmes: entre don, equité et rémunération*. Paris: Éditions L'Harmatton.

British Association of Social Workers (1973) 'The inalienable element in social work', *Social Work Today* **4**(1), 17.

Bruce, T. (1991) *Time to Play in Early Childhood Education*. London: Hodder & Stoughton.

Bruner, J. (1988) *Acts of Meaning*. Cambridge, MA: Harvard University Press.

Bryant, B. *et al.* (1980) *Children and Minders*. London: Grant McIntyre.

Bull, J. *et al.* (1994) *Implementing the Children Act for Children Under 8*. London: HMSO.

Candappa, M. *et al.* (1996) *Policy into Practice: Day Care Services for Children under Eight – An Evaluation of the Implementation of the Children Act, 1989*. London: HMSO.

Casas i Aznar, F. *et al.* (1998) *Primera infancia: demanda social i propostes de treball en els ens locals*. Barcelona: Diputació de Barcelona.

Clark, M. M. (1987) *Children Under Five: Educational Research and Evidence*. London: Gordon & Breach Science Publishers.

Clarke-Stewart, A. (1991) 'Day care in the USA', in Moss, P. and Melhuish, E. (eds) *Current Issues in Day Care for Young Children: Research and Policy Implications,* 35–60. London: Department of Health in association with the Thomas Coram Foundation.

Cooper, A. *et al.* (1995) *Positive Child Protection: A View From Abroad*. Lyme Regis: Russell House.

Cox, M. (1992) *Children's Drawings*. London: Penguin Books.

Curtis, A. (1994) 'Training to work with young children', in David, T. (ed.) *Working Together for Young Children,* 159–69. London: Routledge.

Dankworth, A. (1984) 'Making music', in Fontana, D. (ed.) *The Education of the Young Child: A Handbook for Nursery and Infant Teachers,* 2nd edn, 233–55. Oxford: Basil Blackwell.

David, T. (ed.) (1994) *Working Together for Young Children: Multi-Professionalism in Action.* London: Routledge.

David, T. and Nurse, A. (1999) 'Inspections of under fives education and constructions of early childhood', in David, T. (ed.) *Teaching Young Children,* 165–84. London: Sage Publications.

Department for Education and Employment (1997) *Guidance on Early Years Development Plans and Partnerships.* London: HMSO.

Department for Education and Employment (1998) *Meeting the Childcare Challenge.* London: HMSO.

Department for Education and Employment (1999) *Tomorrow's Children: The Review of Pre-schools and Playgroups and the Government's Response.* London: DfEE.

Department for Education and Employment (2000) *Investing in Our Future: Consultation Pack on the National Standards for the Regulation of Day Care.* London: DfEE.

Department for Education and Employment and Department of Health (1998) *Consultation Paper on the Regulation of Early Education and Day Care.* London: HMSO.

Department for Education and Science and Department of Health and Social Security (1976) *Low Cost Provision for the Under Fives.* London, HMSO.

Department for Education and Science and Department of Health and Social Security (1977) *Combined Nursery Schools and Day Centres.* London: HMSO.

Department For International Development (1999) *Building Support for Development: Raising Public Awareness and Understanding of International Development Issues.* London: DFID.

Department of Health (1991) *The Children Act 1989: Guidance and Regulations.* Volume 2, *Family Support, Day Care and Educational Provision for Young Children.* London: HMSO.

Doyle, C. (1990) *Working with Abused Children.* Basingstoke: Macmillan.

Early Childhood Unit (1991) *Ensuring Standards in the Care of Young Children: Registering and Developing Quality Day Care.* London: National Children's Bureau.

Elfer, P. and Beasley, G. (1991) *Registration of Childminding and Day Care: using the Law to Raise Standards.* London: HMSO.

Elfer, P. and Beasley, G. (1997) *A Law Unto Themselves? A Survey of Appeals and Prosecutions under Part X of the Children Act 1989, Concerning Childminding and Day Care Provision.* London: National Children's Bureau.

Escayola, E. and Odena, P. (1987) *Escola bressol.* Barcelona: Patronat Municipal de Guarderies Infantils.

Fernald, A. (1989) 'Intonation and communicative intent in mother's speech to infants: is the melody the message?', *Child Development* **60**(6), 1497–510.

Fox Harding, L. (1997) *Perspectives in Child Care Policy,* 2nd edn. Harlow: Longman.

Fryer, J. (1985) *Give Your Child The Right Start: The Suzuki Way To Creative Talent.* London: Souvenir Press.

Goldschmied, E. and Jackson, S. (1994) *People Under Three: Young Children in Day Care.* London: Routledge.

Gregory, E. (ed.) (1997) *One Child, Many Worlds: Early Learning in Multi-cultural Communities.* London: David Fulton Publishers.

Gura, P. (1996) 'An entitlement curriculum for early childhood', in Robson, S. and Smedley, S. (eds) *Education in Early Childhood: First Things First,* 136–52. London: David Fulton Publishers in association with the Roehampton Institute.

Heaton, K. and Sayer, J. (1992) *Community Development and Child Welfare.* London: Community Development Foundation Publications in association with the Children's Society.

Her Majesty's Inspectorate (1991) *Aspects of Primary Education: The Teaching and Learning of Music.* London: Department for Education and Science.

Herbert, S. (1999) 'Under fives: directors critical of plans for Ofsted to regulate pre-schools', *Community Care* **1284** 6–7.

Hertfordshire County Council Education Department (1991) *Physical Activity in the Early Years: 3 to 5 years.* Hertfordshire: Hertfordshire County Council.

Hopkins, G. (2000) *An Inspector Calls: A Practical Look at Social Care Inspection.* London: Russell House Publishing.

Jackman, J. (1994) 'Nursery judgement sows confusion', *Community Care* **1023** 6–9.

Jackson, B. and Jackson, S. (1979) *Childminder: A Study in Action Research.* London: Routledge & Kegan Paul.

Jackson, S. (1994) 'Young children in the care system', in David, T. (ed.) *Working Together for Young Children: Multi-Professionalism in Action,* 119–32. London: Routledge.

Keenan, D. (1995) *Smith & Keenan's English Law,* 11th edn. London: Pitman Publishing.

Kinney, L. and McCabe, T. (2001) *Children as Partners: a Guide to Consulting with Very Young Children and Empowering them to Participate Effectively.* Stirling: Stirling Council.

Lane, D. (1996) *Case Review in Respect of HS Born 18th February 1993 Died 25th October 1993: Final Report.* Sheffield: Sheffield Area Child Protection Committee.

Learmouth, J. (1996) 'OFSTED: a registered inspector's view', in Ouston, J. *et al.* (eds) *OFSTED Inspections: The Early Experience,* 53–60. London: David Fulton Publishers.

Lewis, A. (1995) *Children's Understanding of Disability.* London: Routledge.

Lyus, V. (1998) *Management in the Early Years.* London: Hodder & Stoughton.

Makins, V. (1997) *Not Just a Nursery … Multi-agency Early Years Centres in Action.* London: National Children's Bureau.

Malik, H. (1998) *A Practical Guide to Equal Opportunities.* Cheltenham: Stanley Thornes Publishers.

Maw, J. (1996) 'The handbook for the inspection of schools: models, outcomes and effects', in Ouston, J. *et al.* (eds) *OFSTED Inspections: The Early Experience,* 22–32. London: David Fulton Publishers.

McGurk, H. *et al* (1995) *Staff:Child Ratios in Care and Education Services for Young Children.* London: HMSO.

Melville, S. (1997) *Principles of Play Safety,* Paper delivered at National Playing Field Association Conference 20/1/97. London: Playlink Publications.

Morgan, G. (1984) 'Change through regulation', in Greenman, J. T. and Fuqua, R. W. (eds) *Making Day Care Better: Training, Evaluation and the Process of Change,* 163–84. New York: Teachers College Press.

Moss, P. (1991) 'Policy Issues in Day Care', in Moss, P. and Melhuish, E. (eds) *Current Issues in Day Care for Young Children: Research and Policy Implications,* 4–19. London: Department of Health in association with Thomas Coram Foundation.

Moss, P. (2000) 'Foreign services', *Nursery World* **3733** 10–13.

Moss, P. (2001) 'New Labour's record: end of term report', *Nursery World* **3745** 10–13.

Nelson, J. B. (1982) 'The politics of federal day care regulation', in Zigler, E. F. and Gordon, E. W. (eds) *Day Care: Scientific and Social Policy Issues,* 267–306. Boston: Auburn House Publishing Company.

Norvez, A. (1990) *De la naissance a l'ecole: santé, modes de garde et préscolarité dans la france contemporaine.* Paris: Presses Universitaires de France in association with Institut National d'Études Démographiques.

OFSTED (1993) *First Class.* London: HMSO.

OFSTED (1998) *The Quality of Education in Institutions Inspected under the Nursery Education Funding Arrangements.* London: OFSTED.

Penn, H. (1994) 'Working in conflict: developing a dynamic model of quality', in Moss, P. and Pence, A. (eds) *Valuing Quality in Early Childhood Services: New Approaches to Defining Quality,* 10–27. London: Paul Chapman Publishing.

Penn, H. (1997) *Comparing Nurseries: Staff and Children in Italy, Spain and the UK.* London: Paul Chapman Publishing.

Petrie, P. (1994) *Play and Care Out of School.* London: HMSO.

Phillips, J. (1979) *Give Your Child Music* London: Paul Elek Publishers.

Pugh, G. (ed.) (1996) *Contemporary Issues in the Early Years: Working Collaboratively for Children*, 2nd edn. London: Paul Chapman Publishing in association with the National Children's Bureau.

Qualifications and Curriculum Authority and Department for Education and Employment (2000) *Investing in Our Future: Curriculum Guidance for the Foundation Stage*. London: Qualifications and Curriculum Authority and Department for Education and Employment.

Raven, M. (1981) 'Review: the effects of childminding: how much do we know?', *Childcare, Health and Development* **7**(2), 103–12.

Redmond, P. W. D. and Shears, P. (1995) *General Principles of English Law*, 7th edn. London: Pitman Publishing.

Rickford, F. *et al.* (2000) 'Regeneration game', *Community Care* **1349** 23–5.

Rumbold Report (1990) *Starting with Quality: Report of the Committee of Inquiry into the Educational Experiences Offered to Three and Four Year Olds*. London: Department for Education and Science.

Save the Children Fund (1995) *Day Care Regulation and Support: Local Authorities and Day Care Under the Children Act, 1989. Summary by Andrew West of MSS thesis by Steph Petrie*. London: Save the Children.

Scoffham, S. (1999) 'Young children's perceptions of the world', in David, T. (ed.) *Teaching Young Children*, 125–38. London: Sage Publications.

Secretary of State for Social Services (1974) *Report of the Committee of Inquiry into the Care and Supervision Provided in Relation to Maria Colwell*. London: HMSO.

Siraj-Blatchford, I. (1994) *The Early Years: Laying the Foundations for Racial equality*. Stoke-on-Trent: Trentham Books.

Social Services Inspectorate (2000) *Who's looking After the Children?* London: HMSO.

Swann Report (1985) *Education for All*. London: Department for Education and Science.

Sylva, K. (2001) 'Room for the whole child', *Nursery World* **37457** 34.

Sylva, K. *et al.* (1986) *Monitoring the High Scope Training Progam 1984–5: Final Report*. Oxford: Department of Social and Administrative Studies, University of Oxford.

Tonge, W. L. *et al.* (1977) 'Families without hope: a controlled study of thirty-three problem families', in Fitzgerald, M. *et al.* (eds) *Welfare in Action*, 48–53. London: Routledge & Kegan Paul in association with Open University Press.

Troyner, B. and Hatcher, R. (1992) *Racism in children's lives: A study of mainly-white primary schools*. London: Routledge in association with National Children's Bureau.

Valios, N. (1999) 'Under-fives' services are by no means child's play', *Community Care* **1285** 11.

Vernon, J. and Smith, C. (1994) *Day Nurseries at a Crossroads: Meeting the Challenge of Child Care in the Nineties*. London: National Children's Bureau.

Welshman, J. (1999) 'The social history of social work: the issue of the "problem family" 1946–70', *British Journal of Social Work* **29**(3), 457–76.

Whalley, M. (1994) 'Young children in day nurseries and combined centres run by the Social Services Departments – practitioner research', in David, T. (ed.) *Working Together for Young Children: Multi-Professionalism in Action*, 145–58. London: Routledge.

Wiltsher, A. (2001) 'Backbench View', *Nursery World* **37458** 10–11.

Wisbey, A. S. (1980) *Music as the Source of Learning*. Lancaster: MTP Press.

Woodhead, M. *et al.* (eds) (1998) *Cultural Worlds of Early Childhood*. London: Routledge.

Yudkin, S. (1967) *0 – 5: report on the Care of Pre-school Children* London: Allen & Unwin.

Subject index

Author index

Lightning Source UK Ltd.
Milton Keynes UK
18 December 2009

147679UK00009B/31/A